STORIES
of
OLD GLENDORA

STORIES
of
OLD GLENDORA

Ryan Lee Price

Charleston  London

THE
History
PRESS

Published by The History Press
Charleston, SC 29403
www.historypress.net

Images courtesy of the Glendora Historical Society.

First published 2012

Manufactured in the United States

ISBN 978.1.60949.533.6

Library of Congress Cataloging-in-Publication Data

Price, Ryan Lee.
Stories of old Glendora / Ryan Lee Price.
p. cm.
Includes bibliographical references.
ISBN 978-1-60949-533-6
1. Glendora (Calif.)--History. 2. Glendora (Calif.)--Biography. I. Title.
F869.G53P76 2012
979.4'93--dc23
2012003704

This book is dedicated to my children, Natalie and Matthew, in the hopes that they will find the history of the world around them as exciting as I do.

Contents

Acknowledgements

It doesn't seem so, but history is a living being, an ever-shifting and evolving entity capable of changing its tone, face and direction as more and more stories, evidence and facts come to the surface. With the advent of the Internet, the world's archives and personal records, stories and images have become available to anyone patient enough to search for them. Foremost, I would like to thank the countless individuals across the country who have spent their time posting on the web old pictures, stories not often shared and little-known facts about the lesser-known individuals and events that make the history of Glendora so fascinating.

I would like to thank Denise Bresee and Jeffrie Hall at the Glendora Historical Society Museum for their continued support of my research; Sandy Krause at the Glendora Public Library for answering my many questions about the microfilm newspaper archives; and Gordon and Norma Rowley for access to their vast collection of Glendora ephemera and firsthand knowledge about Glendora. Also, I'd like to thank my wife, Kara, and my mother, Linda, for making sure I spelled everything properly.

Most importantly, I'd like to thank you, the reader. By purchasing this book and showing an interest in old Glendora, you are supporting local history.

The Myth of the Charter Oak
of the Pacific

If the town of Alosta in Glendora had survived the real estate burst around the turn of the last century and been allowed to develop on its own, today it would probably resemble the area known as Charter Oak, a largely residential neighborhood split between Glendora, Covina and San Dimas, a community that bridges three cities, each claiming a portion of the neighborhood. Though it is regarded as an official locality by the U.S. government and has its own school district (the first Charter Oak School opened on September 9, 1894, with twenty-four students), it is not an incorporated city or a recognized town but rather more of a borough. In the mid-1960s, Glendora annexed the area north of Arrow Highway, and Covina annexed the area south of Arrow Highway (and San Dimas obtained a few streets to the east). Several small "county islands" of unincorporated area remained within Charter Oak until the 1980s.

However, 130 years ago, the area that would become Charter Oak began in a way similar to every town within a ten-mile radius: as a Mexican land grant, a large ranchero, and then a series of small farms soon to be parsed into town sites, streets and rural communities. The early ownership of Charter Oak followed the same lineage as did Glendora and Azusa, but it never made it as far as incorporation—it was melded into its neighbors.

The neighborhood of Charter Oak in southern Glendora was named because of a story involving buried treasure, a harrowing escape and a similarity to the original Charter Oak in Connecticut.

Its name is derived from a famous tree that once stood three thousand miles away in Hartford, Connecticut, and there is an interesting myth surrounding that fabled tree, one that would capture the imagination of any treasure hunter who heard the story. The official charter to the colony of Connecticut, the organic laws of the land set down by the pilgrims who settled the land, arrived in Hartford, Connecticut, in September 1662.

In 1687, Sir Edmond Andros, then governor of New England, stormed into Butler's Tavern and demanded that the charter be returned to King James II so it could be officially invalidated. During a lengthy debate that was headed toward bloodshed, all of the candles in the tavern were suddenly extinguished. When order was restored to the room, the charter had vanished! Captain Wadsworth had silently carried off the charter and secreted it in the large, hollow tree fronting the house of Samuel

Wyllis, then one of the magistrates of the colony. Forever forward (until it was toppled in a storm in 1856), that tree was known as the Charter Oak.

Now, how that story relates to a little hamlet three thousand miles and three hundred years away in California is a similar tale of buried treasure, a heroic battle and a grand tree presiding over it all; the story of the Charter Oak of the Pacific is established as either local lore or complete fabrication by creative minds, as only the tale itself remains. All possible facts and potential proof have disappeared over time, with very few exceptions.

Rancho La Puente, San Jose and San Jose Addition meet at a singular point marked on official surveys as "S.J. No. 10," and around that corner was founded the village of Charter Oak sometime in the 1890s. To the south of this was a piece of land that used to be called the Hollenbeck Track in the Puente Rancho, part of the forty acres of land originally owned by B.F. Allen (north of Covina Avenue between Sunflower and Valley Center), perhaps from which Allen Avenue gets its name (now regrettably called Auto Centre Drive). After losing a considerable fortune earned in banking, real estate and business speculation in the Des Moines region, Allen came to San Dimas in about 1876 to reinvent himself.

In *The History of Pomona Valley*, written by Frank Parkhurst Brackett in 1920, he told of the myth of the Charter Oak (but credited it to William Hoogendyk) and wrote that the land on which it stood was also owned by a Walter Irving Allen, who was born in about 1846.

After losing a considerable fortune in Des Moines, B.F. Allen relocated to Southern California and purchased forty acres south of Glendora in 1876 to be near his brother, Walter Irvin Allen. Somewhere on the Allen brothers' property, the Charter Oak stands.

Brackett claimed that Walter Allen was the brother-in-law of William Bowring and the neighbor of H.C. Mace, "the only two remaining pioneers in this section of the valley" (at least in 1920). Bowring married Edith Louisa Allen when she was seventeen, and he was instrumental in organizing the Charter Oak Citrus Association on March 13, 1902. Also at the meeting was H.C. Mace, who in 1887 planted an orange grove in Charter Oak and began hauling water in wagons, probably from the San Dimas Canyon two miles away. Other ranchers joined him in cultivating deciduous fruits and olives for the next fifteen years, but none of these attempts proved successful until the land was cleared for citrus orchards.

Since Charter Oak in Glendora didn't get its name due to mere flattery of a tree in Connecticut, how did it get its name then? The story begins in 1847 and ends with an unlikely source.

Toward the end of the Mexican-American War, Commodore Robert F. Stockton rescued U.S. Army general Stephen W. Kearny's surrounded forces after the Battle of San Pascual on December 6 and 7, 1847, and with their combined and resupplied force, members of the U.S. Marine Corps moved from San Diego to the Los Angeles area on January 8, 1847, linking up with John C. Frémont's Bear Flag Battalion (from where California got its state flag design). With American forces totaling 560 soldiers and marines, they fought 150 Californios in the Battle of Rio San Gabriel.

According to the myth, as the Americans fled from the battle at the San Gabriel River, they lost their flag and some valuable papers. San Antonio, the commander in charge of the Los Angeles volunteers who gave the Americans such a great thrashing, was on his way back to Mexico to share in his victory. On the road from Los Angeles to San Bernardino, his group—now joined by two traders heavy with gold—stopped at Cienega, the last source of water until San Bernardino. They camped for the night near some friendly Indians about twenty-five miles east of Los Angeles.

Word spread to the Americans that San Antonio was near. Eager to recapture the flag and the papers, the Americans rode out to search for him and his army. San Antonio, fearing such an attack, helped bury the gold, with the flag and the papers, near a very large oak tree. Just as dusk was near, the Americans attacked, chasing San Antonio into the oak tree, where he remained all night, escaping the next morning back to Los Angeles.

The American soldiers returned to the tree several days later, and holes were dug all around the large tree without success in finding the flag and papers (nor the gold they couldn't have known about). When the search was given up and they were about to depart, one officer remarked, "This indeed is a replica of the old Charter Oak."

The only problem with the basis of this myth is that it isn't true. The Battle of Rio San Gabriel took place in present-day Montebello, and it is historical fact that Stockton and Kearny's troops crossed the river and engaged the Californios in such numbers that it caused the Mexican forces to retreat west toward present-day Vernon, south of downtown Los Angeles, where they again fought the Americans in the Battle of La Mesa.

Four days later, the remaining forces of Californios surrendered to the Americans, ending the war in California. On January 13, 1847, Jose Antonio Carrillo, acting as a commissioner for Mexico, drafted in English and Spanish the Treaty of Cahuenga (a treaty that ended hostilities in California) and was present at its signing on the kitchen table of Tomás Feliz's six-room adobe house at Campo de Cahuenga in what is now North Hollywood, directly across from the main entrance of Universal Studios.

The myth suggests that San Antonio and his forces captured a flag and some papers and that the battle at the San Gabriel River was a disastrous one for the Americans. Instead, the Americans won the battle and gave chase, and the only flag that they may have had with them was the American flag, which was safe with Archibald Gillespie, who was able to raise over the house the same U.S. flag that he had been forced to take down at the war's beginning the year before.

However, details usually become lost in history; let them be overlooked for now. Instead, who is "San Antonio" from the story? It seems logical that the "San Antonio" mentioned in the myth was Jose Antonio Carrillo, as he was instrumental in organizing the Los Angeles volunteers and was second in command under Captain José Mariá Flores at the Battle of Rio San Gabriel and many others over the two years of the war. He was

Though historians have given credit to William Hoogendyk for the origins of the tale, Don Antonio Franco Coronel first related the story of the buried treasure underneath the Charter Oak to Helen Hunt Jackson, who printed it in "Echoes in the City of Angels" in the December 1883 issue of *Century Magazine*.

at most of the battles and seems to be considered one of the leaders, not to mention being instrumental in negotiating the California treaty.

On the other hand, another name comes to the surface, one that seems much more likely, especially considering the true origins of the story: Don Antonio Franco Coronel. Written in the Historical Society of Southern California's magazine *Quarterly* by H.D. Barrows in May 1894 is an account of Coronel's life, one that certainly would earn him the title of "San" ("Saint").

As for the details, let's change the location of the battle from the San Gabriel River to the Dominguez Hills battle. It takes place in October 1846 and not 1847, which would satisfy "San Antonio" leaving for Mexico in the fall. It would also make sense that he would return to Mexico soon after the battle, because Don Antonio Franco Coronel did so in 1846 to receive his commission as aide-de-camp. Also, the American forces were still in the Los Angeles area in great numbers, and after a defeat such as the one at Dominguez Hills, they would likely be interested in some retribution.

Another problem with the myth is that there were no troops in the San Gabriel Valley in the fall of 1847, especially under Kearney, which is a good reason to conclude that the story takes place in 1846. Stockton had set up his headquarters in Los Angeles (where Olvera Street is now) and commanded a small occupying force in 1847, while the bulk of the army, by then, had headed into Mexico to finish the war.

One more small issue is that the first mention of the place name "Charter Oak" doesn't appear anywhere before 1894, when the first school was started there. Odds are good that some random person passing by—perhaps Bowring, Mace, Allen, Collins, Rowland or anyone else who knew their oak tree lore—could have easily made the connection. California was then a mecca for immigrants from back east, and one of these men could have easily come from Connecticut or perhaps read a history book about the thirteen colonies.

California Place Names by Erwin Gustav Gudde and William Bright (1998) noted this: "The community developed in the late 1890s and was probably named because a large oak tree reminded someone of the famous Charter Oak in Hartford, Connecticut. The post office is listed in 1904. There is no evidence to support the local tradition that the place was named when a party of Americans achieved a victory near the oak at some time in the war with Mexico."

But not so fast. The originator of the Charter Oak story is none other than Helen Hunt Jackson, a famous author best known for her book *Ramona*, the 1884 novel about a part-Indian orphan raised in Spanish Californio society with her Indian husband, Alessandro.

Jackson was born Helen Fiske in Amherst, Massachusetts, to Nathan Fiske and Deborah Vinal. Her life could be considered mostly a tragedy. She had two brothers who both died soon after birth, and she got her writing skills from her father, a minister, author and professor of Latin, Greek and philosophy at Amherst College. Jackson's mother died in 1844, and her father followed three years later. In 1852, she married army captain Edward Bissell Hunt, who died in a military accident in 1863. Their son, Murray Hunt, had already died in 1854 of a brain disease, while their other son, Rennie Hunt, died of diphtheria in 1865.

During the winter of 1873–74, while she was in Colorado Springs in search of a cure for tuberculosis, she met William Sharpless Jackson, a wealthy banker and railroad executive. They married in 1875. Interesting to note is that today she is well known as Helen Hunt

Jackson, but she never used that name herself, using Helen Hunt or Helen Jackson instead.

Jackson inadvertently thrust herself into the limelight of Indian affairs after hearing about the cruel treatment of Ponca Indians when they were removed from their Nebraska reservation in 1879. She started investigating and publicizing the wrongdoing, circulating petitions, raising money and writing letters on behalf of the Poncas. She also started writing a book condemning the Indian policy of the U.S. government and noting the history of broken treaties. Called *A Century of Dishonor*, published in 1881, it demanded the reform of policies demonstrating a lack of humanity and justice shown toward the Indians. It was widely ignored, and since her health was declining, she went to Southern California for a much-needed rest. While she was there, she was employed by Century Publications to do a piece on Indian lifestyles.

There, in 1882, she met Don Antonio Franco Coronel, former mayor, city council member and overall authority on early California history. From the *Quarterly*: "Mr. Coronel, in his lifetime, made a most honorable record as a friend of the defenseless Mission Indians of Southern California. Of this fact Mrs. Helen Hunt Jackson has borne warm testimony in several national publications. He gave to Mrs. Jackson the materials of her story of Ramona, and aided her in many ways in acquiring a knowledge of the customs and traditions of the people of the country, necessary to give characteristic coloring to the story."

Jackson listened to his stories, one that included the basis for the Charter Oak tale that appeared in the December 1883 issue of *Century Magazine* under the title "Echoes in the City of Angels." However, no specific tree was mentioned, and Coronel was not around by the time the American officer likened the tree to the original Charter Oak.

From an interview with Coronel's wife, Mariana, in *The True Story of Ramona: Its Facts and Fictions, Inspiration and Purpose*, by Carlyle Channing Davis and William A. Alderson (1914): "Chosen as the bearer of captured American flags to the Mexican capital, Don Antonio was chased all over this country by the soldiers of General Kearney, who was determined that the flags should not be sent [back to Mexico]. Dead or alive, he must be captured, and every inducement was offered the Indians to assist in taking him."

That version is slightly different in that it doesn't mention an oak tree specifically, but it does mention Kearney, the friendly Indian village and the American flags. But the greatest folly of the entire story—as with all fantastic treasure hunting tales—is that it doesn't account for why Coronel didn't come back and dig up the loot. Maybe he did and all that was left was an old tree…or maybe there was no loot to speak of and only an American flag in an old Indian village.

Instead, locals who heard the story apparently littered the ground around the Charter Oak with holes, desperate to find the treasure. After Allen, the land was sold to Westwood H. Collins, who was strongly connected to the Holy Trinity Episcopal Church on Third Avenue in Covina. After he took ownership of the property, he was tasked with filling in the dozens of holes dug around the tree by fifty years worth of treasure seekers in order to plant citrus trees and make a living as a rancher.

It is unclear when after 1886 Collins purchased the Charter Oak tree and its pockmarked land, but by 1920, it had changed hands again and was under the supervision of R.H. Rowland. This Rowland, though he may be a relative, is not the Rowland for which Rowland Avenue in Covina is named (no doubt it's for John Rowland, who bought most of Rancho La Puente in 1841).

After all of this lore and mystery, where did the Charter Oak once stand and what happened to it? The oak, decorated with an ornate sign of the cross carved into its bark, as well as legendary scars from many hangings, has officially disappeared. Originally, it sat northeast of the center of Allen's forty acres, which would have been north of Covina Avenue between Sunflower and Valley Center, roughly where Cienega Avenue and Castleview Avenue cross each other—most decidedly in Covina. There are many claims that the Charter Oak tree still exists on the property owned by brother and sister Rod and Debbie Bakke, on Cienega a few blocks east of Castleview. The family has owned the tree for more than fifty years and recall both scars showing that their tree was used for hangings and a faint carving of a cross, a marking detailed numerous times in the myth. As of 2012, the Bakke tree—infested with borer beetles, sick with root rot and severe dieback—is slated for destruction.

More than likely, this Charter Oak was forgotten and fell victim to the bulldozer in the name of urban sprawl and progress.

So is it true? Who really knows, but the next time you find yourself at the corner of Cienega and Castleview (or in front of the Bakkes' house), look around for an oak tree with a cross carved on its trunk…or perhaps a majestic stump of a once impressive oak tree. Underneath that you may just find a fortune. Or perhaps Kearney's torn and tattered battle-scarred twenty-eight-star American flag. Either way, it's still treasure.

The Smudge Pot

From the 1939 book *California: A Guide to the Golden State* (from the Federal Writers Project):

> *On every cold night in winter, the grower must be ready with his orchard heaters. The heaters in commonest use are oil-burning stack pots, which are placed between the tree rows, one to a tree. With the broadcast of a frost warning, the watchman in charge of an orchard stays up all night, keeping crews ready to light the heaters with gasoline torches resembling an engineer's long-spouted oil can. The burners must be watched and regulated at intervals. Where the smudge pot heating method is used, a thick blanket of black smoke produced by the fuel protects the trees from frost. Threat of frost is greatest about an hour before sunrise. During a cold period, everything within miles—clothing, furniture, faces—is covered with the greasy soot.*

The citrus industry resulted in a variety of then modern inventions, from refrigerated cars, specialized packinghouses, individualized tools for picking, sizing, cultivating and pruning the trees to shipping crates, box makers, sorters and packers, not to mention the many developed techniques for pruning, irrigating, cultivating and plowing. But the one

On an especially cold night, the valley would glow from the blazes of thousands of smudge pots.

invention that perhaps outranks them all is the orchard heater, otherwise known as a smudge pot.

The term "orchard heater" is perhaps a slight misnomer, as the smudge pots don't directly heat the trees themselves. It would be impossible to create a fire inside a smudge pot that would have enough heat to properly maintain a warm temperature for a tree let alone a group of trees. Instead, the smudge pot's main purpose is to create a blanket of smoke that hangs over the entire orchard, and that smoke creates a barrier that retains radiant heat from the earth.

The scientific phrase for this phenomenon is aptly called the "Smudge Pot Effect," as pointed out in Mark Z. Jacobson's 2002 book, *Atmospheric Pollution: History, Science, and Regulation*. "During day and night all aerosol particles trap the Earth's thermal-IR radiation, warming the air. This warming is well known to citrus growers who, at night, used to burn crude oil in smudge pots to fill the air with smoke and trap thermal-IR radiation, preventing crops from freezing."

Every winter between 1924 and 1956, local ranchers and orchard owners could tune their radios to KFI on the low end of the radio dial to await the frost report. The original station first went on the air in 1922, started by Earle C. Anthony in his garage, and today, KFI is the radio station most listened to in the United States. Interestingly enough, the F and I in its call letters stand for "Farmer's Information."

In an article entitled "I Remember Earle C. Anthony," Newcomb Weisenberger, an engineer who had worked at KFI for thirty-three years (from 1947 to 1980), wrote: "Earl C. Anthony was born on December 18, 1880. In 1897 he built a working electric car. Becoming interested in radio, he constructed a 50-watt transmitter on a breadboard and began broadcasting as KFI on April 16, 1922. His primary business was as a California Packard distributor which was located at Wilshire and LaBrea in Los Angeles."

The voice of the local weather from 1924 to 1956, Floyd D. Young's radio addresses at 8:00 p.m. on KFI told local citrus ranchers estimations of the dew point and the lowest temperature predicted for the various regions.

At 8:00 p.m. on KFI, the slow monotone voice of meteorologist Floyd D. Young would inform all of Southern California about the various conditions of the weather, including his estimations of the dew point and the lowest temperature predicted for the various regions (the frost warnings were moved to 7:00 p.m. until the late 1970s, when they were discontinued altogether).

So important were the frost reports to the citrus industry that every other form of news and entertainment crossing the airwaves from KFI (which was affiliated with NBC at the time) was halted at 8:00 p.m. Then, as KFI radio engineer Newcomb Weisenberger explained in his article "The KFI Pioneer's Preemption," "When the KFI announcer at the Vermont studios in Los Angeles introduces the weatherman, Floyd Young, I will pull this small lever down, disconnecting the program line that has served KFI listeners all day. This includes the Red Network of the National Broadcasting Company! NBC hasn't stopped programming! Mr. Anthony and Southern California have stopped listening! This is a double throw switch. Not only will my movement of the lever cutoff all lines to the transmitter. It will connect Floyd Young directly, bypassing everything else!"

Weisenberger continued: "We all knew the consequence of throwing this little switch. We were aware of the contrast between NBC's Chesterfield Supper program and Floyd Young's dusty little report of uninteresting numbers, for little places, miles away. People still tell me how they hated losing the music of Paul Weston with Jo Stafford and the celebrity guests, when KFI cut away."

From a January 1, 1945 article in *Time* magazine: "Bald, middle-aged Floyd Young, who broadcasts weather news in a dreary, ticktock, statistical monotone, is quite a radio favorite in Southern California. If he goes over his allotted time, Los Angeles station KFI cuts out its NBC network show until he finishes. Nightly, he gives the temperature lows expected, and forecasts the time of their arrival in farm communities. The fruit farmers all listen. If he announces, 'Cucamonga, 31 degrees, 5 a.m.,' Cucamonga's farmers set their alarms accordingly, light their smudge pots and save their trees. Broadcaster Young has also acquired a large following among women: if his news is bad and smudges are indicated, they bring in the wash."

Claude A. Cole was in charge of the Fruit Frost Service for the San Gabriel Valley District. He observed the various instruments (as well as those in the field) and helped forecast the evening's temperature range and possible frost points.

Young worked from his office in Pomona, and as the regional director of the U.S. Weather Bureau, he organized the Fruit Frost Forecast program in 1917, four years after the Great Freeze of 1913, during which nearly 60 percent of all the citrus orchards in Southern California were destroyed. Temperatures dropped to ten to fifteen degrees Fahrenheit in some areas, representing some of the coldest nights ever measured in the state.

Also onboard with the program was Claude A. Cole in charge of the Fruit Frost Service for the San Gabriel Valley District from his home in Covina. There he observed the various instruments (as well as those in the field) and helped forecast the evening's temperature range and possible frost points. The information was sent to Young (who also observed his own measurements), as well as to the various exchanges via teletypes and telephones.

Following the 1913 freeze, many studies were conducted and publications printed regarding the effects of frost on citrus orchards, especially concerning the art of forecasting the weather. *The Standard Cyclopedia of Horticulture* by Liberty Hyde Bailey (1915) explains:

It is not possible to forecast frost twenty-four or thirty-six hours in advance without the aid of the weather map; but, by observing the local conditions during the late afternoon and early evening, it is possible often to determine whether a frost will occur before morning. Assuming that it is the frost season, the conditions to be considered are: (1) the character of the preceding weather; (2) the state of the sky, whether cloudy or clear; (3) the direction and force of the wind; (4) the trend of the temperature; and (5) the atmospheric pressure.

These were the local conditions that Young and Claude A. Cole were observing and reporting directly to the farming community each night.

After Young listed the expected critical low temperatures and dew points of most every town where citrus orchards grew in Southern California (although, according to Pflueger's *Glendora*, "Young never mentioned the area where the one-time largest fruit packing house was located"), the work was on for the ranchers, who sometimes had to stay up all night to make sure that the smudge pots stayed burning. Schools were sometimes closed during really bad freezes so the children could help with the smudge pots throughout the long nights.

A copyright search shows that literally hundreds of orchard heater patents and designs filled the Patent Office from the 1890s until the 1970s, such as Plank (No. 944,745, December 28, 1909), Hamilton (No. 976,072, November 15, 1910), Johnson (No. 1,024,633, April 30, 1912) and Scheu (No. 1,536,692, May 5, 1925). Scheu is perhaps the most famous company to produce smudge pots used in Southern California, as it is the very familiar Hi-Lo Heater produced by Scheu Products Company in Upland and Los Angeles—and owned by inventor William Scheu—that has populated many orchards over the years. They had a variety of styles, from a square barrel and a short stack to the most-produced tall stack with a re-breather vent pipe on the side of the chimney that forced some of the nonburned fuels back down into the chamber to make for a more complete combustion. The filler caps generally had a three- or four-hole flue control valve.

The concept behind smudge pots and orchard warming is much, much older. According to the 1914 *Encyclopedia of Practical Horticulture* by

Granville Lowther and William Worthington, "Although much interest has been manifested in the prevention of frost-injury to orchards in recent years, it is well known that the protection of plants and fruits from such injury dates back more than 2,000 years. Pliny the Elder, one of the most noted of Roman writers, who lived from 23 to 79 AD, states that the Romans practiced heating and smudging as a protection against frost-injury."

In Helen Kennard Bettin's book *This I Remember*, Mrs. C.C. Warren wrote: "In 1898 and 1899, there was a heavy freeze which severely damaged the lower parts of the groves. Mr. Huber had already attempted frost control by burning coal in buckets under his trees. Mr. Warren could not 'see' putting money into the newly invented 'smudge pots' but Mrs. Warren invested the whole of a $400 gift, which came to her, in these pots. Mr. Warren also bought them at a later date."

Speaking of Helen Kennard Bettin, the smudge pots must have been an important aspect in her family while she was growing up, as they certainly left a lasting impression on her, evident in a report that she wrote for school. There is no year on the report (though there is a very fancy colored drawing of a flaming smudge pot), but this might have been written while she was in high school (it is labeled English 10, and she graduated from high school about 1907).

Perhaps as a precursor to her interest in writing, she wrote about her family's experience with the smudge pots:

My father donned a warm coat and with a flashlight, stepped out into the darkness. We waited. The telephone rang. To my disappointment, my younger sister won the dash race to the phone— "Frost Warning—28 degrees in your grove." My father returned. Again he donned his hat, coat, and gloves. Stirred by the excitement that filled the air, I put on an old dress, boots and, after a frantic search, found some old gloves...The departure, including a hop, skip, and jump, came, my father "to save the grove," and I to make a general nuisance of myself peering into the gloomy depths of the unlighted smudge pots. Enthusiastically lifting off the tops, I watched my father light them with the torch, heard them hiss, roar,

A typical scene on a frosty night, a group of boys prepared to weather the storm and keep the smudge pots lit all night.

and sputter, saw them spurt flames of fire, blaze and glare, and make many fantastic figures with flames. Tired out with toil, I sat beside one and gazed at the weird forms of smoke and flames. Presently my father returned, looking like a demon from Hades, covered with smudge.

The culture of the citrus industry seemed to transcend age, and a soot-covered face became a badge of courage among boys, meaning that you had been up all night, braving the elements to help save the family farm, or that you had weathered out the storm to make a living for yourself. For her article "The Grove Experience: Smudging All Night Long" in *LaVerne* magazine, Jen Newman interviewed Dr. Dwight Hanawalt, LaVerne College class of 1941 and professor of physical education emeritus at ULV, and Daryl Brandt, LaVerne College class of 1952, both having worked the smudge pots when they were children: "'There was no problem telling who the kids had been that had smudged the night before. Their eyes would be all dark,' tells Hanawalt. The black around the eye was not only the soot attracted to moist areas, but from lack of sleep. They returned home looking like they had spent time in a coal mine. 'Smudge soot would be in your hair, ears, and nose and all over. When you'd blow your nose, it would be black,' Brandt accounts."

There are two types of frost (which should be distinguished from a freeze, in which the moisture on the inside of the plant becomes solid), both generally known as radiant frost, in which the frost occurs as a result of losing heat from the surface of the plant. A "hoar frost" occurs when water vapor is deposited onto the surface and forms a white coating of ice, which is what most people would call frost. However, a "black frost" occurs when the temperature falls below zero degrees Celsius and no actual ice forms on the surface of the plants. If the humidity is sufficiently low, then the surface temperature might not reach the temperature at which ice frost will form. When the humidity is high, ice is more likely to deposit, and a hoar frost can occur. Because heat is released during the ice deposition process, hoar frosts usually cause less damage than black frosts.

In a lengthy discourse in the 1895 *Yearbook of the United States Department of Agriculture*, early methods of keeping away the frost in citrus orchards are discussed: "On still nights, when the temperature barely reaches 32 degrees Fahrenheit, it is often possible to prevent frost injuries by making a smudge, thus covering the field with a haze, which prevents the rapid loss of heat. Dense smoke can be produced by burning wet straw, wet leaves, sawdust, etc. A mixture of two-thirds sawdust and one-third gas tar makes an effectual material for forming a smudge."

Unfortunately, all the preparation in the valley won't stave off the inevitable frost, as was seen during the winter of 1937. The freeze was so severe that *Time* magazine wrote an article about it in its February 1, 1937 issue: "Temperatures had been low for a fortnight in Southern California when one afternoon last week the Federal Fruit Frost Service sent out a warning that during the night the mercury would dive farther below freezing than it had for 24 years." This, of course, referred to the 1913 freeze. "Frantic men with torches went rushing through the citrus groves lighting great smudge pots, from which billowed smoke to protect the trees from frost. Before morning, temperatures in many places had fallen through the 18-degree mark set by the 1922 freeze which ruined half the citrus crop. A second night of low temperatures followed. Traffic crawled and tangled on the darkened roads, while hundreds of oil trucks were given the right of way, carrying fuel to the smudges."

An article in the *Glendora Press* on January 7, 1949, broke down the costs of running smudge pots: "To adequately protect an orchard during such an extreme cold, 50 smudge pots per acre are needed. Each of these consumes nine gallons of oil per night. At a cost of $0.10 per gallon, such an acre would cost in the vicinity of $45 each night for the oil alone. In addition, the cost of labor must be added to this depressing total. Rates of $1.25 per hour were the minimum in the Glendora area."

Former KFI engineer Weisenberger wrote:

> *My father cultivated and produced oranges commercially. We sat close the radio tuned to KFI. What Mr. Young said would determine whether we went to bed or stayed up all night! Thousands of other growers and tens of thousands of workers listened too. This army of men might soon be carrying their flaming torches through the groves, dripping splashes of burning oil into the waiting orchard heaters. The following day tanker trucks would be ready to deliver oil to replace that burned away. There would be railroad tank cars on the sidings to re-supply these trucks.*

As time marched on, the citrus industry began to falter. Ecology was on the rise. Clean air became increasingly important to an ever-growing community. In 1945, the Los Angeles Board of Supervisors designed a position called the director of air pollution control and banned the emission of dense smoke from all factories. H.O. Swartout, then the Los Angeles County health officer, suggested that pollution was coming from other sources besides big business. In 1946, Raymond R. Tucker was hired by the *Los Angeles Times* to suggest ways of cutting the pollution problem. Tucker came up with twenty-three ways to reduce air pollution, including the suggestion to create a countywide air pollution agency, eliminating backyard incinerators and smudge pots among them.

Tanks like these dotted the San Gabriel Valley, filled with oil ready to be doled out to the thousands of smudge pots that would blanket the freezing sky with soot.

In the fall of 1947, Louis C. McCabe, director of the newly formed Los Angeles Air Pollution Control District, appealed to Southern California citrus growers to abolish the soot and smoke from more than 4 million orchard heaters. A headline for an article in the October 20, 1947 *Pasadena Star-News* called out "Asks Citrus Growers to Cut Smoke…Anti-Smog Chief Says Pall Not Needed." McCabe and agricultural authorities launched a campaign to educate growers on how to operate heaters so that they prevented frost damage to crops but didn't belch out black clouds.

In 1950, the Orange County Air Pollution Control District adopted a regulation prohibiting the use of dirty fuels, including old tires and used motor oil, in smudge pots. They also banned the smokiest smudge pots, which included garbage pails. Finally, in 1958, smudge pots were completely banned in all of Los Angeles County.

Starting in the early 1950s, growers began using wind machines in place of smudge pots. A large propeller mounted on a tower mixed pockets of cool and warm air in orchards, effectively raising temperatures at the ground and preventing frost damage. The wind machines were more expensive to buy but more cost-effective over a period of years because they didn't have to be constantly tended.

An article for the South Coast Air Quality Management District sums up nicely the history of smudge pots: "Today, residents might still see the rusted hulk of a smudge pot lying in an orange grove, serving as a reminder of a bygone era and a polluting nuisance put in its place by clean technology."

Why Is There a
Compromise Line Road?

It is a street name that is begging for an explanation. What compromise? Who compromised, and what exactly did the compromising parties come to terms with? It is easy to guess that the compromise was in the form of a boundary line that formed the basis for a new road. But which one? There were countless scuffles in this area, from Dalton's initial partition of his property to land development around the turn of the twentieth century.

There are only four known stories of how Compromise Line Road got its name: *The Glendora 100th Anniversary* book, Bettin's *This I Remember*, Brackett's 1920 *History of Pomona Valley* and Jackson's *Beautiful Glendora*. And three out of the four have a different explanation. Which one is right?

Until 1834, the land that surrounded Compromise Line Road and what would be Glendora fell under the jurisdiction of the fourth mission in a chain of twenty-one, founded on September 8, 1771, by Fathers Pedro Cambon and Angel Somera. Officially named San Antonio de Padua and San Gabriel Mission, construction on the church itself didn't begin until 1779, but when it was completed, the mission controlled much of the land from Los Angeles to San Bernardino.

In 1834, the Mexican government, fresh from its break from Spanish rule, deemed the Spanish missions unnecessary and made their vast

At the intersection of Route 66 and Compromise Line Road once stood this impressive oak tree, gnarled and trampled by time. It is possible that this oak was the Botello Oak, one of the boundary markers for Dalton's Rancho San Jose.

holdings of land available to the public. Large swaths of it were granted to special Mexican citizens for the return of favors to the government in exchange for colonization of the land.

When the weather began to warm in the spring of 1837, Ygnacio Palomares and Ricardo Vejar trekked to the Pomona Valley to see for themselves the possibilities in the east. Palomares and Vejar named the land San Jose in honor of Saint Joseph, as March 19 (the day they first saw Glendora) is the feast day for the saint. Eight days later, the two men filed a petition with Governor Juan B. Alvarado for "the place being vacant which is known by the name San Jose, distant some six leagues, more or less, from the Ex-Mission San Gabriel." Without much fanfare, the petition was approved by the ayuntamiento (city council) of Los Angeles and granted to Palomares and Vejar.

Simply enough, the two men divided the land equally and arbitrarily: Palomares took possession of the northern half, which became known as Rancho San Jose Arriba (Upper), and Vejar settled in the southern

34

half, which became known as Rancho San Jose Abajo (Lower). Later that year, on August 3, Jose Sepulveda, acting as the mayor of Los Angeles, ordered a survey of the lands to map out the boundaries of the rancho. Lacking solid landmarks, the surveyors used what was available to mark the boundaries: items like a skull inside the boughs of an oak tree or wooden crosses set against the rocks would come back to haunt them years later when the land claims came into question by the United States government.

Enter Luis Arenas in 1838, serving with Palomares in Los Angeles city government and eventually becoming his brother-in-law. On March 14, 1840, Arenas was granted a league of land to be attached to the Rancho San Jose, and the deed was regranted to include Arenas as the third partner with Palomares and Vejar. Arenas took possession of a 4,430-acre rancho known as the "San Jose Addition" but built his house near his brother-in-law at the intersection of McKinley and Gibbs Avenues in Pomona (it no longer exists). His livestock grazed on land that would someday be known as Glendora.

On November 8, 1841, Arenas received another league of land adjacent to Rancho San Jose Addition. It was called Rancho El Susa,

In 1844, Henry Dalton purchased Jose Arenas's 4,431-acre Rancho El Susa and the San Jose Addition for $7,000. This is the view looking east toward Glendora from his home on Dalton Hill, roughly where Sixth Street and Cerritos Avenue meet in Azusa.

which consisted of 4,431 acres. Arenas received the land by a grant from Governor (pro tem) Manuel Jimeno. In 1844, Henry Dalton, a native of England, bought both ranchos belonging to Arenas for $7,000. He chose Rancho El Susa as his home, renaming it Azusa de Dalton, and built a house there on a place known as Dalton Hill. The Dalton home site is near Sixth Street and Cerritos Avenue in Azusa.

The following year, Henry Dalton convinced Ricardo Vejar and Ygnacio Palomares to request a formal partition of Ranch San Jose—that is, Dalton wanted to know exactly what land was his as opposed to what land was Vejar's or Palomares's. Palomares was reluctant at first, but curiosity got the better of him and he agreed to the partition. Judge Juan Gallardo was the mayor of Los Angeles at the time, and he hired surveyor Jaspar O'Farrell to map out the divisions of the two ranchos. It took him five days to produce the map that Judge Gallardo approved on February 12, 1846.

In Frank Parkhurst Brackett's 1920 book *The History of Pomona Valley*, he described the conflict that arose:

> *Between the original owners there had been no trouble, no thought of separation, no question of boundaries. The San Jose de Arriba was Palomares; the San Jose de Abajo was Vejar's, and the "Addition" was Arenas. There were no fences and the cattle were separated from time to time, as they must also be from those of other herds, at the rodeos, by their brands. But after Arenas had sold out his interest to Henry Dalton, the question of division arose. Palomares objected to the partition and protested against the division proposed.*

Not surprisingly, Ygnacio Palomares was not satisfied with the results. For years, he disputed the findings of the O'Farrell survey in a series of legal battles. It was the first of many legal battles to be fought over this property, but did this one in particular result in the great compromise that created the street's name?

The first official survey of the three ranchos was completed by Jasper O'Farrell in February 1846. It clearly shows the boundaries of the three properties, but the big difference is that the O'Farrell survey does not include Rancho Azusa de Dalton, only his Addition property. The upper

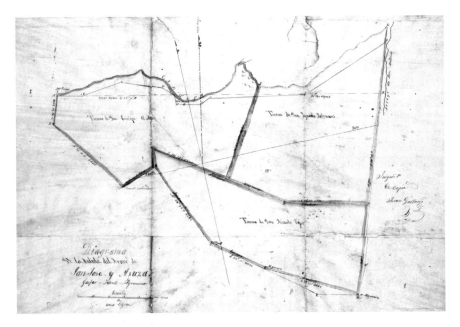

The first official survey of the three ranchos owned by Palomares, Vejar and Dalton was executed by Jasper O'Farrell in February 1846 to show the exact boundaries of the properties.

left-hand corner of the survey begins at San Felipe Hill, better known today as the site of the Fairmont Cemetery.

Two versions of the O'Farrell survey still exist: one is the full document submitted to Gallardo, showing all three of the properties owned by the three men and their relation to one another, while the other one appears to be a copy of the original specifically for Vejar (which he spells with a B), as it only shows his sectioned portion of the land.

Even though the basis of Compromise Line Road has its origins in Palomares's complaints about the survey, a closer look at the O'Farrell survey reveals that the border is too far to the south. However, the angle of Compromise Line Road is a near exact match to the joining border of Palomares's San Jose Abajo and Vejar's San Jose Arriba.

According to early descriptions of their properties, the line dividing San Jose Abajo and San Jose Arriba started at roughly one block or so north of today's Holt Avenue in Pomona. At about Huntington Boulevard (just west of White Avenue in Pomona), the dividing line diverted to the northwest, skirting the west banks of Puddingstone Reservoir (which, of course, wasn't there at the time) and on to the northwest corner of the rancho, where the boundary line crossed Bonita Avenue.

Is the O'Farrell survey wrong? There is very little to go on—some arbitrary descriptions of nonexistent landmarks, a hand-drawn map that may lack some technical accuracy and no record of Palomares's official complaint. But what of the road itself? Compromise Line Road, at the point where it intersects with Valley Center, follows a twelve-degree delineation south of true east all the way until it meets Route 66, which follows the same angle as far as Garey Avenue in Pomona before it turns due east again.

The reason it works out like this, according to a 1921 Glendora map produced by O.A. Gierlich, is that Alosta (at the time) did not go all the way through directly like it does today. Instead, it met up with Compromise Line and Valley Center to form a three-way triangular intersection. From there, Compromise Line Road took cars out of town

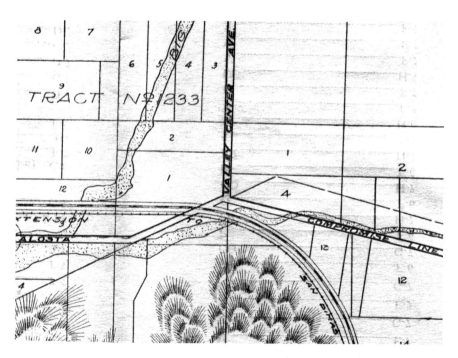

On a map produced by O.A. Gierlich in 1921, the configuration of the streets before the Santa Fe overpass was built in 1929 shows that Compromise Line Road extended from Valley Center to well beyond Lone Hill into San Dimas.

to the east. It probably wasn't until 1929. when the Santa Fe Railroad built the overpass, that Alosta was straightened, bypassing Valley Center altogether and canceling out most of Compromise Line Road in its place.

In Frank Parkhurst Brackett's 1920 book *The History of Pomona Valley*, he described the boundaries of the San Jose Addition:

> *The San Jose Addition is a five-sided piece, of irregular shape, one side of which coincides with the sixth side of the Rancho San Jose between the corners of the Tinaja and Botello Oaks. Another side runs north of west from the corner of the Botello Oak to the much disputed north corner, southeast of Glendora. This corner was marked by an oak which parties living to the north attempted again and again to burn or destroy, so as to push their south line farther south. There was much dispute over the corner, but finally it was located by formal agreement, and the road which follows the new line from the Botello Oak corner to this one, has since been known as "Compromise Road."*

The confusion of the landmarks is very evident. Tinaja? Botello Oak? Looking at the O'Farrell survey, those landmarks are not mentioned, and it is well assumed that those two trees are no longer around. But they are mentioned quite frequently in numerous publications. However, this unnamed oak tree in Brackett's book is intriguing. It seems to coincide with the Botello Oak.

Sheldon Jackson weighed in about Compromise Line in his book *Beautiful Glendora* when he discussed the boundaries of the Addition, per the adjusted Hancock survey, but he left the road's origins decidedly vague:

> *The northwest corner of the San Jose Addition, as finally settled, was near what is now the intersection of Gladstone and Ben Lomond avenues and from there it ran diagonally, skirting the north side of the South Hills, to a point a few hundred feet north of the present Santa Fe Railway viaduct which crosses Highway 66. From this point (the present road is significantly called "Compromise Line Road," and extends from the end of Valley Center Avenue to Highway 66*

Before the Santa Fe overpass was built in 1929, Route 66 made a northerly jog just east of Hunter's Trail before it continued east again, meeting up with Compromise Line Road on the opposite side of the tracks.

just east of the viaduct) it traveled diagonally once again almost parallel to Highway 66, and then hooked onto the main body of the San Jose Rancho.

Additionally, there have been two conflicting reports published in two credible books about Glendora in the last twenty years. The evidence, although not pointing to a specific conclusion, suggests that the Jackson book erred in crediting the Compromise Line Road to the wrong generation of ranchers in Glendora.

First, *The Glendora's 100th Anniversary* book lists street names and their apparent origins on page 176, claiming that Compromise Line Road was a result of a boundary dispute "between Rancho Azusa and the San Jose Addition (1850s)."

There was only one survey done in the 1850s, and that was by the now infamous Henry Hancock in 1858, when he split up Dalton's land, moved the Addition about two miles to the east (so Rancho Azusa de Dalton and the Addition were no longer touching) and opened up most of the Azusa Valley to renters, squatters, homesteaders and/or settlers.

Second, on page 76 of the well-respected *This I Remember* by Helen Kennard Bettin, a story written by Leslie A. Warren (the son of C.C. Warren, who lived on property very close to Compromise Line Road) talks about the road and the "Bar T" oak:

> *The Bar T oak stands at the intersection of Compromise Road and Route 66. It is—or was—marked with a bar and a "T." It served as a landmark in the early days. When Mr. Joy bought the present Warren land, he wanted the disagreements settled between the San Jose Ranch Company south of Highway 66 and the ranchers north of 66. So both sides ran a survey—and disagreed. Finally, a compromise was agreed upon and the present line of Route 66 established.*

C.C. Warren and family came to Glendora in 1898, bought a seven-acre tract of land from F.D. Joy on the corner of today's Amelia and Route 66 and set up a two-room house. In addition to Joy, his neighbors were Harvey Davenport, Stoddard Jess and Charles Cunningham. Five hundred acres of land in that area had been previously owned by Joy, Jess (who was the president of a bank in Pomona) and a third, unknown man. In Bettin's *This I Remember*, Mrs. F.D. Joy wrote in November 1945 about Compromise Line in the vaguest of terms: "It was through the efforts of Mr. Joy and Mr. Warren that 'Compromise' Road, off our present Highway 66, was gotten through."

This provides, at the very least, a timeline of Compromise Line Road, if Bettin's book is to be taken as first-person fact. Both Joy and Warren purchased property between 1898 and 1900, and they are given credit for creating the road; Compromise Line Road itself shows up (maybe for the first time) on a map printed in 1921.

What happened in those twenty-two years? From whom did Joy buy his property? Furthermore, Leslie Warren's story supports the ideas found in Brackett's book that a tree was instrumental in deciding the boundary line—perhaps the oaks mentioned in both books are, in fact, the same oak tree. The problem is discovering where, exactly, this elusive Botello Oak used to stand and if it is in line with the current configuration of Compromise Line.

On the Hancock/Thompson/Wheeler compilation survey map, there is no mention of a Botello Oak. However, at the southeast corner of Hancock's version of San Jose Addition, marked on the map on Old San Bernardino Road (which is now Arrow Highway) at the corner of the Addition and Rancho San Jose proper, is "Place of the Encino Del Tenaja." This, in conjunction with the descriptions of the Tenaja and the Botello Oak in McKinney's book, as well as Brackett's book, places the Botello Oak roughly where Baseline meets Route 66 just east of San Dimas Canyon Road. Brackett's description is worth mentioning again: "Another side [of the San Jose Addition] runs north of west from the corner of the Botello Oak to the much disputed north corner, southeast of Glendora. This corner was marked by an oak." On any map of the Glendora/San Dimas border area, follow Route 66 from the Baseline intersection in San Dimas toward Glendora; it goes directly to Compromise Line.

What is most interesting, perhaps even the crux to this story, is that shown in the photograph of Route 66 looking west past Compromise Line Road is a giant old live oak on that very corner; it's so big, in fact, that it obscures Compromise Line Road as it meets with Valley Center and Route 66. It is quite an imposing landmark. There is very little doubt that the oak tree Brackett is referring to and the "Bar T" oak in Warren's story—the unnamed oak that makes the southern line of the San Jose Addition (according to the Hancock survey because it was the accepted rule of thumb by then)—are the same, making it logical that Leslie Warren's story about a more modern boundary conflict between the San Jose Ranch Company and ranchers who owned the northern property is the most probable.

A extra note is worthy of mention here. Explore the Glendora region in any modern Thomas Guide (1996 and 2001 editions specifically) and you'll see that the Thomas brothers still hold a candle to the Hancock survey by including the boundaries of the Rancho San Jose Addition, which follows just north of Compromise Line. Also, look at the 1921 O.A. Gierlich map. The dotted line that peaks just northeast of the Valley Center/Compromise Line Road junction is also the Hancock-surveyed San Jose Addition line.

If there was a compromise that led to the formation of this road, it no doubt involved this line and the San Jose Ranch Company.

By 1863, Rancho San Jose was in decline, hit hard by a smallpox epidemic that killed or scared off most of the settlers. The following year, on November 8, Palomares himself became ill and died. Drought soon followed, cattle died and crops withered. Ricardo Vejar, up until then one of the wealthiest men in the state, was forced to borrow money to keep his rancho, but it wasn't enough. Late in 1863, unable to repay a $30,000 loan, he turned his section of the San Jose (the lower half) over to creditors. He died in poverty in Spadra in 1882.

The American businessmen and creditors who foreclosed on Vejar's land were Isaac Schlesinger and Hyman Tischler. But neither man was ever given the chance to take possession of the land. Tischler was ambushed by vengeful Mexicans, and his partner, Edward Newsman, was killed. It was enough for Tischler, who was plenty frightened for his life, to flee to San Francisco to manage the property from afar. Additionally, Schlesinger (while embezzling $25,000 in gold) was killed aboard the *Ada Hancock* just off the Banning Docks in Wilmington on April 27, 1863, when the boiler exploded from a wayward bullet aimed at Schlesinger.

With Schlesinger dead and Tischler too scared of Vejar to return, German-born Louis Phillips was in charge of the property, receiving a quitclaim deed from Tischler for the rancho in exchange for $30,000. Phillips, in turn, sold some land to William Rubottom, who named his new land Spadra after his hometown of Spadra Bluffs, Arkansas. It later became Pomona. The Palomares family sold seventy acres to Robert S. Arnett in 1868, and two years later, Cyrus Burdick bought land in what would become Ganesha Park. In 1873, Reverend Charles F. Loop and Alvin R. Meserve purchased two thousand acres of Palomares land in the northwest section of the rancho for eight dollars per acre. This land is situated about three miles northeast of Pomona and is perhaps known locally as the Loop and Meserve Tract.

Because of his heavy debt resulting from the extensive legal action protecting his land, Dalton was ironically forced to sell the Addition property indirectly to the Mound City Land and Water Association in 1878. Technically, he deeded half interest in his four ranches to

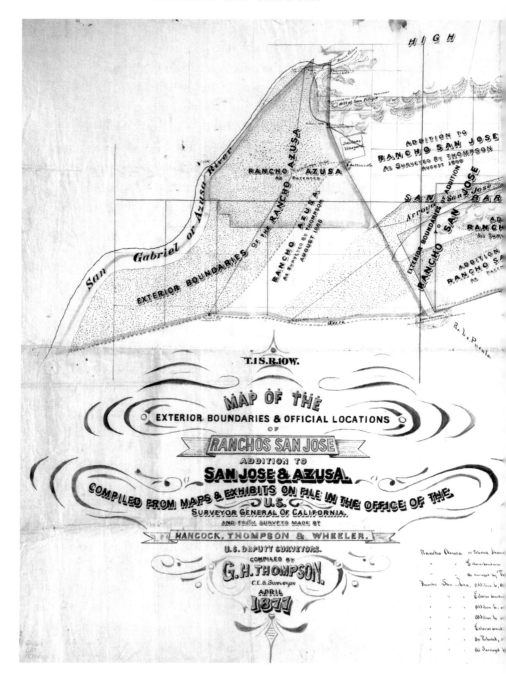

In 1877, George Thompson was commissioned by the U.S. Deputy Surveyor's Office to map the boundaries of the Ranchos San Jose, Azusa and San Jose Addition. Known as the "Compilation Map," it shows possible location of the Botello Oak in relation to Compromise Line Road.

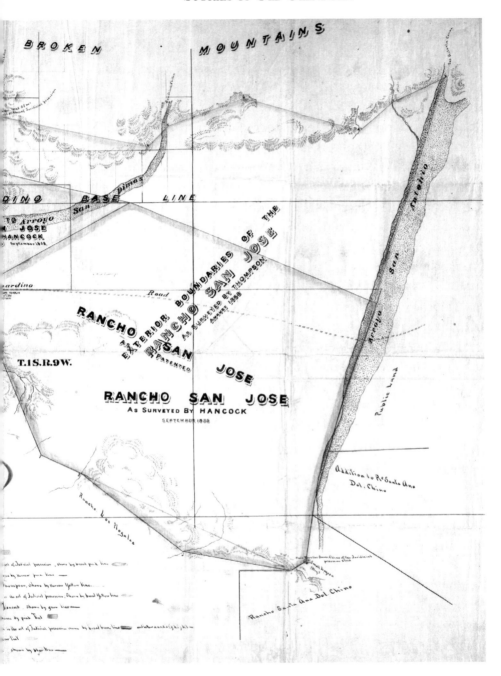

Francois L.A. Pinoche, and when he died in May 1874, his heirs foreclosed—this is the source of Dalton's major legal problems. In the end, on January 27, 1877, Dalton's attorney, Louis Wolfskill, took over the debt on the property. Enter the Mound City Land and Water Association, incorporated on July 25, 1878, with a capital stock of $200,000. Soon thereafter, Wolfskill and Dalton signed over everything to the Mound City Land and Water Association.

A year later, what was left of the Mound City property ended up on the auction block. Beckett elaborated: "In the next five years, the four great ranches of thousands of acres were tossed back and forth like a basketball...deed after deed was made out for the whole property, and mortgages were assigned and reassigned, with amounts at issue running from $1,000 to $100,000. Wolfskill to Cardwell, Daltons to Sabichi, the Pinoche executors to J. Mora Moss, and then to Martz and Martz, everybody by the sheriff to the Los Angeles County Bank."

From this new development, C.T. Mills and Moses L. Wicks (both from the Pomona Land and Water Company) formed a new company that included some Santa Fe officials and several from the Mound City Land and Water Association. Some of the largest stockholders were M.L. Wicks, George W. Hughes, R.F. Lotspeich and F. Sabichi, along with about thirty other men in the valley. The company was named the San Jose Ranch Company and was incorporated on February 28, 1887, receiving most of the property held by Slauson and those of the Mound City Land and Water Association. Additionally, it bought 665 acres at the northwest corner of Louis Phillip's half of the San Jose Rancho, thereafter possessing most of the land north of the San Jose Hills (those above Cal Poly), from LaVerne to Glendora and onto the Azusa ditch; basically, the San Jose Ranch Company controlled all of the San Jose Addition and all of Dalton's portion of the Rancho San Jose, nearly 8,000 acres.

From here, the San Jose Ranch Company ran into conflict with the San Jose Land and Water Company over control of the land in and around the San Dimas Canyon and points west. They weren't interested in the land, just the water under it. Dozens of lawsuits resulted, including some visits to the Supreme Court. In the end, most of the original founders of each company filtered off to start their own water companies (as such was the real money at the time), all coming together in 1911 to form the San Dimas Water Company. The land in question fell to various settlers as it was sold off in bits and pieces over the course of several years.

Brackett stated:

> *After two years on the Chino, Mr. Burdick decided to have a ranch and cattle of his own* [in 1868], *even if on a small scale. In the San Dimas Canyon, north of Mud Springs, there was living at this time a Dr. Charles Cunningham and his family, who had come from San Bernardino not long before and taken up a quarter section of government land. He called Mr. Burdick's attention to a part of a section between his land and that of Henry Dalton in the addition to the San Jose Tract, near the mouth of the San Dimas Canyon…Thus it came about that he selected for his ranch the place on which is now the C.C. Warren house and grove. Here they built a dwelling house, barn and milkhouse.*

The following year, Burdick sold his ranch to the Cunninghams and moved south to the Ganesha Park area.

The only two credible mentions of the origins of Compromise Line Road are by the wife and son of one of the permanent settlers in the immediate area, C.C. Warren, who owned the land on the corner of what is now Route 66 and Amelia Avenue.

Here's where the story ends. Warren and Joy (with others perhaps) disputed the boundaries of their properties along a borderline that would become Compromise Line Road sometime between 1898 and 1921.

After all of this, what is left to tell about Compromise Line Road? Nothing but the fact that it is still there and that the historic sources on this topic have been exhausted. On one side of the road live the Warrens, the Joys and the Cunninghams, and on the other, controlling interest lies with the San Jose Ranch Company. All were at odds over the borderline that revolved around the unfortunate placement of a grand oak and how it relates to their lands.

Citrus

The First Union High School?

A source of Glendora's pride is its education system, as it has long endeavored to create a solid educational foundation for the children in the town; it has been that way ever since the city's inception.

An interesting claim that has surfaced time and again is that Citrus Union High School—a joint high school for Covina, Glendora and Azusa—was the first such establishment in California. The claim only adds to the pride that Glendorans feel about their schools—that we have the distinction of being on the forefront of the educational system in California. But is it true?

Citrus Union High School was officially founded on July 14, 1891, but was it the first in the state? Two other schools in California also make the claim that they were the first union high school in the state: Livermore High School (formally Livermore Union High School) in Livermore to the east of San Francisco and Elk Grove Union High School in Sacramento County.

High schools as a whole were nothing new. In 1856, the first public high school in California was founded in San Francisco on Powell Street between Clay and Sacramento. For two years, it was called the Union Grammar School (because of the combination of grammar and high school) and, in 1858, became the San Francisco High School. George Washington Minns,

By the early 1900s, attendance had improved greatly, and the need to expand had become an issue. The new facility was designed by George F. Costerison and built by Charles Harper for $12,990.

a Harvard graduate, was the first principal; the following year, he founded Minns' Evening Normal School, a school for training teachers, and then went on to help found San José State University in 1870.

The first high school in Los Angeles was built on the corner of Temple and Broadway in 1873. Six years later, the revamped California Constitution called for a halt on public money spent for high schools, effectively ending any prospects for rural children to go to high school. John Swett noted in his 1911 book *Public Education in California*: "The upward pressure of the elementary schools, growing stronger and stronger, led to the passage of a state law (1891) whereby contiguous common-school districts could unite to form a union district and establish a union high school, and thereafter the number of high schools was rapidly increased."

That law went on the books on March 20, 1891, officially allowing the formation of union high schools, but which one was first: Citrus, Livermore or Elk Grove?

After the first building was blown off its foundation and destroyed on December 11, 1891, classes were moved to the Ed Haskill building at the northeast corner of Citrus and Gladstone avenues. In the summer of 1892, Citrus School District purchased Thomas Smith's house and shoemaking shop, where classes were taught for the next eleven years.

It is a well-established fact that Citrus Union High School was founded on July 14, 1891, sourced directly from Alfred Paul Clark's *Citrus Speaks* (1994), as well as Floyd Hayden's *History of Citrus Union High School and Junior College*. In Clark's book, he quoted William Bryant Cullen, one of the high school's founding trustees, who wrote in the 1903 Citrus annual: "An election was called on the 14th day of July, 1891, for said purpose [to form a union high school] in the different districts concerned. The result of the election was 103 votes cast—93 in favor and 10 opposed to it. The school was named the Citrus Union High School and has the distinguished honor of being the first Union High School formed in the State of California, for which she now holds the banner presented by the State Superintendent of Schools."

The first schoolhouse owned by the Citrus Union High School District was used for classes from September 1892 to December 1903 before moving to the buildings on Dalton Hill. It was located at the northeast corner of Citrus and Gladstone. During the first year of 1891–92, the high school was housed in two different rented buildings, the first of which was blown down in a storm on December 11, 1891.

According to the Sacramento County Office of Education, "The Elk Grove Union High School, established in 1893, was the first Union High School in California. It opened with 20 students and one teacher, Mr.

Robertson R. McKissick." Its 1893 start date is two years after Citrus and Livermore, and therefore it could not possibly have been the first union high school in California.

Livermore's claim that it is the first union high school in the state is slightly more difficult to dispute, and a barrage of differing facts eventually comes to light. From the Livermore High School website, which tells a whitewashed history of its school:

> *Mr. F.R. Fassett, who was one of the leading citizens of Livermore and served in the State Legislature in 1890, introduced a bill which allowed any township to establish a union high school. Livermore established its high school which was opened in 1891 with E.H. Walker as teacher and principal in one of the rooms of the Livermore Grammar School. The Class of 1894 was first to graduate from Livermore Union High School. The contract for the first high school building was agreed upon December 31, 1892. The building consisted of eight rooms and was finished in the summer of 1893 on the site of what is now a Livermore Area Parks and Recreation District Facility.*

According to the *California Blue Book, 1850–2000*, the assembly representation for Alameda County (where Livermore is located) in 1890 was not Fassett. F.R. Fassett didn't serve in the assembly until 1895, as he was elected on November 6, 1894, and only served one term. Therefore, he couldn't have been instrumental in passing the education bills that formed the union high schools in the state.

In an article titled "Our Pioneer High School," Phillip Holmes made an assertion that is a little more difficult to dispute: "The California State Legislature adopted a Union High School law in 1890 to provide for high schools in rural areas. Lida Thane led a petition drive to secure a high school in Washington Township. The petition drive was successful and local residents voted September 12, 1891, to form Union High School No. 2. Livermore had already voted to form district No. 1, so ours was No. 2." Union High School No. 2 became Washington Union High School, which is now on the state registry of historic places.

According to the history section on the city of Fremont's website, "Building Union High School No. 2 at Centerville in 1892 became the greatest cultural, social, and economic force in the township. It was the hub of activities that joined people of all ages throughout the township. Students came from all eight towns to attend their high school. Generations of graduates went out to work in Washington Township with strong ties to their school."

If Washington Union High School was the second union high school in the area, that means that Livermore Union High School was the first… or at least the first to vote to form a union high school.

This leads to an interesting bit of information from *Past and Present of Alameda County, California*, from the S.J. Clarke Publishing Company in 1914: "In September 1896, the Union high school at Livermore opened with a total of forty-four students, which number was later increased to nearly sixty. Principal Connel was in charge of the school."

The trustees from Glendora and Azusa voted to form Citrus Union High School on July 14, 1891, three months after the law took effect. School would not officially start until late September 1891, when students

This is the picture of the class of Citrus Union High School in 1894, taken in front of the second schoolhouse located in the town of Gladstone at the corner of Citrus and Gladstone avenues. There were only four graduates that year: Helen Clapp, Herman Lee, May Griswold and Ina Reeves. The teacher, Isabelle Owens, is seated in the window.

met at an old hotel built by Larkin Barnes on the southwest corner of Gladstone Street and Citrus Avenue.

Roughly at the time Citrus was first in session, September 12, 1891, the folks in Centerville voted to start a union high school, but they recognized that their neighbors in Livermore had already voted to start a union high school; therefore, they felt it necessary to name their union high school Union High School No. 2.

Past and Present of Alameda County lists the trustees of the high school: "The trustees of the Livermore high school in July, 1891, were F.R. Fassett, Fred Hartman, J.C. Martin, Al. Clark, J.L. Banggs, A. Fuchs and J.G. Young; the latter was chairman. They concluded to open the high school in the public school building at Livermore."

The final answer comes in the form of a history article by Livermore High School alumnus Jason Bezis: "The election creating Union High School No. 1 of Alameda County was on July 6, 1891, just eight days before the Citrus Union High School vote."

Even though Citrus Union High School is the second union high school in the state, that doesn't make it any less special to the thousands of students who gained a better life as a result.

Charles Silent and His Mountain Retreat

There is a short list of people who played an influential role in the building of Glendora in the twentieth century, and the name that tops the list is Judge Charles Silent, a man about whom little is known, despite the authority and influence that he imposed during the pivotal year of 1911, when Glendora became a city. But then again, helping to develop cities was nothing new to Silent; he had been doing such things most of his adult life.

Almost every biographical listing for Charles Silent notes that he was born in Germany in 1843, the exception being the 1880 United States Census, which lists him as being born in Ohio from German-native parents. According to the unpublished 1933 manuscript of Lamberta Margarette Voget called "The Germans in Los Angeles County California 1850–1900," Silent's family didn't move to the United States on their own accord but instead fled here in 1848, "his father having participated in the revolution." This is verified in C.F. Lummis's book, *Los Angeles and Her Makers*. Specifically, it can only be imagined how involved his father was, especially since the revolution, called in Germany the March Revolution, began in his hometown of Baden-Baden and spread east, but it was enough to cause him to leave the country for America that same year.

Once in America, because of the poor financial status of his family in Columbus, Ohio, Charles was out of the house on his own by the age

HO

Fill-In puzzl
delightful di'
answers! Y
the diagr
across ar

The a
ac
I

Win
$100!
See page 148

PENNY'S ❋
VORITE
L-IN™

NTENTS

of thirteen. He made his way to New York City on borrowed money and caught a ship bound for San Francisco via an overland road on the perilous Panama Isthmus.

Once in San Francisco, in August 1856, Silent settled in Drytown, a small hamlet in Amador County at the base of the Sierra Madres, about fifty miles east of Sacramento in the middle of gold country. It got its name not from its lack of alcohol (quite the contrary—in its heyday, the town boasted twenty-six saloons) but because it is situated on Dry Creek. The following year, the gold from the town's many mines began to run out, and most of the entire town burned to the ground in a suspicious fire. Few people remained to rebuild, but among them was Charles Silent, who stayed for another five years. He spent every available minute in study, as it became clear to him that he wanted to eventually become a lawyer. In the meantime, in 1860, he earned his teaching credentials in the form of a first-grade certificate and taught for two years in the Williams School District at the very school in Drytown where he earned his education.

Two years later, Silent was accepted at the California Wesleyan College in Santa Clara, an institution of higher learning founded by the California Supreme Court in 1851 and now known as the University of the Pacific.

One problem for Charles Silent was that he couldn't afford college. He had to drop out before the end of his first year, but conveniently enough, he was elected principal of the Santa Clara Public Schools, and this allowed him to continue his law education while making a comfortable living. Here in 1864, perhaps in connection with the Methodist church or the university itself, Silent met and married the daughter of Reverend John Daniel of Santa Clara.

In 1867 or 1868, roughly at age twenty-five, Silent was admitted to the bar and began practicing as a junior member of the law firm of Moore, Laine and Silent in San Jose. In the same year, Silent got his first taste of developing real estate. Wrote J.P. Munro-Fraser in his 1881 book *History of Santa Clara County, California*, "In the month of February, 1868, a franchise was granted to S.A. Bishop, Charles Silent, Daniel Murphy, D.B. Moody and others to construct a horse-railroad between San Jose and Santa Clara. S.A. Bishop, John H. Moore, Charles Silent,

Charles Silent was born in 1843 and made a name for himself first as a lawyer, then as a judge in Arizona and, most impressively, as a land developer in Southern California. He retired in Glendora in about 1900 and created Los Alisos, a popular garden oasis for his family and Glendora residents.

Hiram Shartzer, B. Bryant, and D.W. Burnett, organized and were elected Directors, with S.A. Bishop as President."

It was called the San Jose and Santa Clara Horse Railroad Company, and work was first started on August 31. The cars made their initial trip on November 1 from First Street in San Jose to Main Street in Santa Clara, traveling three and a half miles. In 1869, the line was extended eastward along Santa Clara Street to the Coyote Creek Bridge and then afterward to McLaughlin Avenue. In 1887, the company obtained a franchise from the city and county and constructed an electric railroad, which was the first of its kind ever built on the West Coast.

During this time, in 1869, Silent ran for the Republican seat in the California Senate in Santa Clara County. What prompted his foray into politics is a mystery, but perhaps he saw himself at the top of his game and well connected enough in society as a successful lawyer, a real estate developer and a husband to the daughter of an influential reverend. As political races go, it was close, but in the end, his opponent, Charles Maclay, took the win with 2,125 votes to Silent's 1,957.

After that, Silent remained with his law firm for only another year, until 1870, the same year his wife of six years died. It is not known how she died, exactly when or even if his leaving the law firm was a direct result. But what is known is that for the next eight years after 1870, he concentrated on real estate development, a hobby that stayed with him for the rest of his life.

It didn't take him too long to find a new wife, and in 1872, Charles married Mary Tantau, the eldest daughter of Matthew Tantau and Catherine Theuerkauf, mildly successful farmers in Santa Clara. This same year, his old alma mater, California Wesleyan College in Santa Clara, awarded him an honorary master's degree in law. According to *An Illustrated History of Los Angeles County California*, published by the Lewis Publishing Company, "After two years of extensive and lucrative practice with that firm [Moore, Laine and Silent] he severed his connection with it, and until 1878 divided his time between his profession and other pursuits."

Exactly what these pursuits were is not known, but they must have been successful and impressive, at least enough that he was recognized by the presidential administration of Rutherford B. Hayes and appointed one of the three associate justices of the Supreme Court of the Arizona Territory in 1878. A February 12, 1878 article in the *New York Times* confirms Hayes's nominations, which were sent to the Senate for approval the following day. Along with Judge Alfred Noyes and another unnamed judge, Silent was headed for Prescott, while his wife of two years stayed behind in Santa Clara.

In addition to his judicial duties, Silent couldn't deny his latest undertaking, real estate investing, as his name shows up prominently in *The Arizona Diary of Lily Frémont, 1878–1881*, as well as being mentioned in the autobiography by Jessie Benton Frémont (*The Letters of Jessie Benton Frémont*): "[Silent] had left his family in San Jose and resided alone in Prescott. Lily noted that he had a standing invitation to dine with the Frémonts and he literally became JCF's silent business partner. Like Moses Sherman, he, too, would prosper and move on to California."

Silent's actions in Arizona were few. He was involved in some mining, but little else is known aside from his apparent partnership with Frémont. In 1880, he resigned his judicial position and set up a practice in Tucson, Arizona, where he led a very profitable business for three years. In 1884, at the age of forty-one, he retired and moved back to San Jose to be with his wife, Mary.

In 1885, he moved to Los Angeles and shortly thereafter formed the law offices of Houghton, Silent & Campbell with partners Alex Campbell and S.O. Houghton (other partners included Stephen M. White and former governor Henry T. Gage). In the end, however, his continuing to practice law in San Jose, Arizona and Los Angeles became merely a means to an end. After 1887, he was more and more interested in the development of land, the speculation of real estate and the improvement of residential tracts.

While in Los Angeles, Silent ran into a friend from Arizona, Nathan Vail; the two had been introduced by Walter Vail, Nathan's nephew, who with Herbert Hislop bought the 160-acre Empire Ranch near Tucson.

Though Charles Silent had designs for a Craftsman-style house penned by the now famous Charles and Henry Greene, there is no evidence that it was actually built. Instead, Silent and his family of four more than likely lived in a smaller house to the west of these guest bungalows.

It was later discovered to be situated on a large vein of silver, and with Empire Ranch money, Walter Vail was instrumental in incorporating Huntington Beach and building the pier.

Uncle Nathan Vail, a sea captain from New Jersey, was one of the first land developers in Los Angeles, having bought his first seventeen acres of land on the north side of Adams Street, just west of Figueroa. There Vail built a two-story farmhouse and began investing in land around the city. He partnered with Silent on several investments around Los Angeles, and Vail sold his Adams Street house to Silent on November 5, 1885.

One of the two major investments that Silent and Vail were involved with was the development of the Centinela-Inglewood Land Company, established by Daniel Freeman (who owned nearly all of Centinela Valley) to develop the town of Inglewood. According to *Historic Adobes of Los Angeles County* by John R. Kielbasa:

> *The Centinela-Inglewood Land Company initially named the development Centinela Colony. The residential lots were priced between $200 and $750 apiece. Farmland was offered at $200 to $400 an acre, and fine orchard property was listed between $600 to $1500 per acre. Centinela Colony was one of the most successful of the land boom subdivisions with the developers procuring over $1,000,000 in capital by 1888.*

In 1888, the Centinela-Inglewood Land Company merged with land promoters from Redondo, the second of Silent's major investments in Los Angeles, and reorganized under the name of Redondo Beach and Centinela-Inglewood Land Company. All lots for the young town were occupied, and two business blocks were completed. The name of the town was changed from Centinela to Inglewood, named for Daniel Freeman's Canadian hometown.

The following year, the land boom flattened, causing Judge Silent to sell his interest in the two companies to two entrepreneurs from Oregon, J.C. Ainsworth and Captain R.R. Thomas, who completed the development of the harbor. Redondo Beach flourished as the main port for Los Angeles before the federal government built a breakwater at San Pedro.

Over the next few years living in the Vail House, Charles and Mary Silent had two boys, Chester in 1885 and Harold in 1896 (in Azusa, but more on that later). With nothing much to do and nothing important to invest in, Silent decided to break up his own property and subdivide it into exclusive residential houses. To do so, he needed to move the original Vail House on Adams Boulevard to the very rear of the property. Then Silent extended Vail's original driveway from Adams Boulevard north to Twenty-third Street and renamed it Chester Place after his son. On either side, he developed twenty-three 70- by 110-foot lots behind a gated entrance. He built houses on some parts of the property for sale and sold bare lots to anyone who could afford them (in 1901, oil tycoon Edward Doheny purchased a 10,000-square-foot Gothic mansion for $125,000). Nearby at 2345 South Figueroa lived Jonathan Slauson, who went on to found Azusa.

The profits from the Chester Place subdivision prompted Silent to leave Los Angeles and consider leading the rest of his life in a more subdued fashion pursing his interests in horticulture. Incidentally, Silent's house survived and is now part of the twenty-acre Chester Place campus of Mount St. Mary's College.

There are no facts or witnesses to call on to prove why he chose Glendora, but one theory can be suggested: Silent came to Glendora because of his Los Angeles neighbor Jonathon Slauson, the man who developed Azusa. Slauson was living on Figueroa Street in 1880 when he purchased the property in what would become the town of Azusa, and he was neighbors with Silent for about two years before founding Azusa, time long enough for Silent to make acquaintances with another real estate speculator. Another fact, more evident, is that Harold, Silent's second son, was born in 1896 in Azusa, leading one to believe that Silent and his family were in that city as a friend of Slauson's or as an interested land buyer.

It isn't known for certain when Silent permanently arrived on the outskirts of Glendora, but by roughly 1905 (more than likely a few years earlier), he had purchased one hundred acres of land north of Sierra Madre and west of Grand Avenue with an interest in creating Rancho Los Alisos, a parklike setting surrounded by perfectly placed plants and trees, along with a thriving citrus operation. There Silent began to develop his lands into a home. He built thatch-roofed guesthouses for the many

Gertilda and Claus Peterson and their son, Harold, taken in front of their thatched-roof quarters on the Silent Ranch. Claus was the gardener who attended to the dozens of acres of carefully cultivated plant life that made Los Alisos such a beautiful place.

people he entertained throughout the rest of his life. Planned in 1908 (but never built) was Silent's extensive and lavish ranch house designed by Charles and Henry Greene, architect brothers from Pasadena famous for their "ultimate bungalows," exemplified by the popular Gamble House.

Here in Glendora, Silent entered into its social and political circles (which went hand in hand in such a small town), and though there are few mentions of him in the history books of Glendora, it is known that he was influential during the city's incorporation in 1911 and urged its citizens to wait until Foothill was paved by the county before incorporating, to avoid the cost. Silent is given credit for planting the palm trees along Azusa Boulevard because his guests were sometimes inclined to travel to his house that way, and in 1908, the Pacific Electric made stops at Los Alisos specifically for the judge.

Silent's appreciation of city parks was evident at Los Alisos, as his grounds were open to the public, and it wasn't uncommon for Glendorans as well as Azusans to include in their weekend plans a stroll through what would be known as Silent's Park. To make those grounds as nice as possible, Silent employed many people on his property, including Gertilda and Claus Peterson. Peterson's granddaughter, Trudy Sorenson, wrote: "My grandfather worked for Judge Silent as a gardener. They lived in the thatched roof building. My father tells me that Claus took Judge Silent's team of horses and wagon each week into Glendora to buy the weeks' supply of wine."

Sadly, Judge Charles Silent's life wasn't without tragedy. His son, Chester, graduated with a law degree from Stanford and spent the summer of 1907 on the family property in Glendora before going back for postgrad work. On September 20, 1907, Chester Silent vanished. Search teams from as far away as Los Angeles joined local police and even Chester's Delta Tau Delta fraternity brothers in the search. The October 3, 1907 edition of the *Stanford Daily* reported on his discovery: "There was nothing until fraternity brothers Walter H. Hill and Ross W. Harbaugh borrowed a boat to explore Felt Lake. Discovering that the boat leaked, they noticed another one floating near

A snapshot of the Silent sons, Harold and Chester, in the summer of 1907, a few short months before Chester accidentally killed himself while duck hunting on Felt Lake near Stanford.

shore some distance away, and in examining it, found Silent's body. The back of the skull and the left side of the face were blown off. Doctors examining the body decided that the fatal shotgun blast came from the left side below the face. No firearm was found."

In November, the sheriff drained the lake and found Silent's double-barreled shotgun. Examination showed that the right chamber had misfired and that the left chamber had discharged. The sheriff theorized that Silent had pulled the right trigger and, when the shell misfired, examined the weapon, discharging the left barrel.

In his later years, Charles Silent's largest hobby was that of horticulture, and he prided himself on his property and the many plants that grew there. Wilson Popenoe, from the Department of Agriculture, visited Silent's property in 1914 and "became interested in this persimmon tree," he wrote in the *Inventory of Seeds and Plants Imported by the Office of Foreign Seeds and Plants*. "We have at last found the long-looked-for male Kaki Persimmon tree, which should be planted in every orchard of Kaki Persimmons as a pollinator."

On May 14, 1915, a meeting was held for the Ahuacate (Avocado) Growers club at the Hotel Alexandria, and Silent served on its board, probably one of the last institutions with which he was directly involved. After Silent passed away in 1919, F.O. Popenoe (Wilson's father) wrote in the California Avocado Association's Annual Report for 1919: "Judge Charles Silent was regarded by the members of this association as a solid, cornerstone friend. I am sure the members of the board can never forget the pilgrimages made to his beautiful foothill home, the Rancho del Aliso, near Glendora. These pilgrimages were red letter days to everyone privileged to make them."

Silent's land fell out of the family's hands and into those of developers years after his death. The bungalows are completely gone, as are all of his cherished plantings, but his name lives on in Silent Ranch Drive, a street located roughly where his ranch once stood.

Sadly, the people now living on Silent Ranch Drive probably attribute the name to refer to how quiet the street is rather than to a man who helped change the course of not only Santa Clara, San Jose, Arizona and Los Angeles but also the little town of Glendora as well.

Glendora's Famous Map

During the period from 1850 to 1890, many artists were employed by major eastern lithographic firms to produce bird's-eye views of the new towns springing up in the West. Companies centered in San Francisco, of which Britton & Rey and A.L. Bancroft & Company were the largest, soon entered this lucrative field.

The hand-drawn Glendora promotional map is quite a popular one—unquestionably recognized by most anyone familiar with local history—as it has been displayed prominently at the Glendora Library for years (originally it was used in the lobby of a bank on Alosta and Glendora Avenues until it was procured by then deputy city manager Culver Heaton to be displayed at the library), and most of the modern historical accounts use it in some way to show what Glendora looked like soon after George D. Whitcomb carved out the town site in 1887.

What is not widely known is that there are technically three versions of this map: two drafts of an early rough sketch and one polished version of the second draft. Although they are all generally identical in that they show the buildings and streets of the infant town, they do share many specific differences that make each version unique. And there are a few mistakes worthy of note.

Although it is sometimes mistakenly called a Cleland illustration, the original drawing was completed by Edwin S. Moore in January 1888. By 1886, Moore had made a name for himself as an artist specifically tailored to the promotion of the land boom, and over the next five years, Moore drew nineteen views similar in style to Glendora's, all but three depicting towns and cities in California.

From *Views and Viewmakers of Urban America: Lithographs of Towns and Cities* by John William Reps: "Moore lived in Los Angeles at this time; at least his name appears in the city directory for 1888 with an address at 11 Schumacher Block. Either he moved or traveled extensively, for in 1888, he drew views of Bakersfield and Merced and, in the following year, Grass Valley. His three Oregon views, of Ashland, Salem, and Grants Pass, are either dated 1890 or can be assigned to that year."

At the bottom of the map, it notes, "View taken when six months old," which would could mean two different dates: one, six months after the land sale in April 1887 (that would mean that it was drawn in October 1887), or two, six months after the town's official map was recorded with Los Angeles County on September 22 (which would mean that it was drawn in March 1888). Since it is known that Moore was in Oregon for most of the year, perhaps January 1888 is accurate and the "six months old" figure was an estimate.

John William Reps added, "His lithographs, therefore, help to document a fascinating period in the region's development. At least two of his views in this category were published by the land companies responsible for the existence of the communities they depicted."

The Glendora Land Company and the Coronado Beach Company were the two examples of land speculators that paid to have the maps printed for promotional purposes. Whitcomb, no doubt, oversaw the creation of the Moore map and then paid to have it distributed around California in the hopes of attracting attention and new landowners to Glendora. Perhaps these first versions of the map were drawn in haste, Whitcomb longing to get them into the hands of potential land buyers and Moore eager to get to Oregon for another job. Whatever the circumstances, the early version of the Glendora map is rough, with hardened sketch lines, almost similar to a woodcut print of thirty

This is the original version of Glendora's promotional map. It was commissioned by George D. Whitcomb and drawn by Edwin S. Moore.

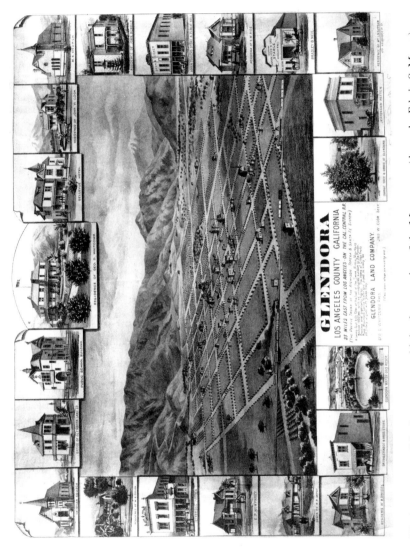

Having a more polished appearance, this is a later version of the Moore map (drawn by Edwin S. Moore), not only showing more realistic details but more than a few changes.

years earlier. Reps dismissed his attempts as an artist by criticizing his attention to detail: "It is unconvincing in its handling of topography, and it is mechanical in execution." Streets don't properly line up—Whitcomb Avenue becomes a jagged stretch of road—trees and bushes are scribbles of lead and all of the elements lack a focused definition.

On the first version, there are no streets named above Leadora, and Vista Bonita doesn't line up with Whitcomb's house at the head of the street. However, on both versions, Wabash is mostly illegible.

The second version is polished and shaded, with darkly outlined features, and it shows a higher degree of exactness to the detail. The dog-eared portions of the map are drawn with realism, the streets have been straightened and the pepper trees are more uniform and regular. Trees have an element of care and realism, and they almost appear larger and more mature, as if time has passed (a specific example is the difference between the trees right above the sixth car on the Santa Fe). It was also reproduced by a professional publisher that specialized in creating lithographs of exactly this kind of work. In the bottom corner of each of the maps—even the rough one—it shows that it was distributed in lithograph form by H.S. Crocker & Company out of San Francisco.

There is no record of the dealings of this company at that time, so it can only be surmised that it began reproducing the original Moore drawing while another artist was busy fine-tuning Moore's work for a later printing. The difference between the two is phenomenal when you begin to study the details. Perhaps H.S. Crocker & Company desired to create a better product, so it had the original redone, adding some details and subtracting others. This is why there are technically three versions of the map: the early version drawn by Moore and printed by him and Whitcomb; the early version drawn by Moore but printed in lithograph form by H.S. Crocker & Company; and the retouched version probably remastered by someone other than Moore and also printed by H.S. Crocker & Company.

H.S. Crocker, who would soon become the president of his company, arrived in California on the cusp of the gold rush on August 13, 1850. Six years later, he started H.S. Crocker Company Printers in a tent in Sacramento and purchased the first offset lithographic press manufactured in America (it is currently in the Smithsonian). A small sign stood outside the tent promising "first class printing" to all customers. The company soon moved to San Francisco, built a five-story plant in 1885 and was considered to be the finest commercial printing establishment in the West.

More than 150 years later, H.S. Crocker & Company is still known for its outstanding printing; however, there were a few problems associated with the Glendora map. Though most faults probably fall to Moore and the original version, a few slipped into the second printing. Following is a list of anomalies and peculiarities associated with each version of the map, as well as with the two compared to each other.

The mysterious Ohio Avenue, centered halfway between Pennsylvania and Grand Avenues, is on no other map ever produced for Glendora, including Whitcomb's own plat map. According to his map, Pennsylvania is the western boundary of his property and the town.

Above Sierra Madre are listed two streets that appear on no other known map of Glendora, including Whitcomb's original plat map (the two streets show up but are unnamed). Oakwood and Summit Avenues

Many of Glendora's original buildings in this 1903 photo, from the Glendora Grammar School to the Glendora Land Company Office, can still be seen.

no longer exist in Glendora. Summit is now Crestglen, going from Vista Bonita to Banna; however, Oakwood has been enveloped into the neighborhood and has disappeared.

No single locomotive in 1888 was capable of pulling seven passenger cars, as shown on the maps, but this might have been an exaggeration to subconsciously convince potential buyers that so many people were headed to Glendora that they needed seven cars attached to every locomotive to handle the influx. Also, notice that the first two cars in the new version have been changed to freight cars. Also, whoever remastered the original for the second version thought it necessary to add "Santa Fe R.R." over the tracks where they cross Carroll.

There are ten small buildings on the northeast corner of Ada and Ohio that disappear in the new version.

In the older version, the Bellevue Hotel is smaller and not accurately drawn.

The building on the northwest corner of Michigan and Bennett Avenues switches sides of the street in the newer version.

On the southwest corner of Virginia and Minnesota, a cluster of houses is replaced by a stand of trees in the new version.

In the older version, it appears as though Minnehaha is spelled wrong (with an "s" in place of the last "a").

In the inset of the "Public School Building," an extra chimney has been added on top of the far-right gable. In the next frame, on the left, the man standing in the doorway of the Land Company Building (Whitcomb himself maybe?) has gone missing in the second version. In the "Jefferson Patten" inset, the people in the image grow shorter in the second version.

In the new version, Meda Avenue no longer goes through to Pennsylvania. Instead, it stops at Vermont, and that is strange because Meda has always gone through to Pennsylvania. What's more interesting is that the lighter shading used to cover up the street is still visible.

Jefferson Patten's store, the first lot sold in Glendora, is mistakenly drawn in the second version on the southeast side of Michigan and Bennett Avenues when it should be where the First Christian Church is now located. He did own several properties, however.

Of course, the largest mistake on both versions of the map is that in the upper-left corner panel, Christian is misspelled, lacking the "h."

However, the largest clue on the map in relation to the accepted history of Glendora is the presence of the Santa Fe Depot, accurately drawn as it was originally constructed. Assuming that the map is correctly dated, and that it shows Glendora as it looked when it was roughly six months old, when exactly was the depot built? Most Glendora historians place the build date sometime early in 1888, claiming that a boxcar was used for the first year of operation. Specifically, Ruth Pratt Kimball wrote in "Glendora—Its History" that "[b]y March of 1887, the railroad was operating two daily trains." This must mean that the depot, as depicted in Moore's sketch, was literally brand new, arguably one of the newest buildings in the drawing.

And here you thought it was all the same map.

George E. Gard,
the Villain

History has made a villain out of George Edwin Gard. He stands for everything Glendora was not in 1887. From this, he has emerged from the pages of Glendora's history books as a money-grubbing bandit who took advantage of a volatile real estate market in the late 1880s, only to line his pockets with cash to make his escape. In his wake, his short-lived town of Alosta was left in ruins, mostly abandoned to melt back into the weeds and eventually be enveloped by its northern adversary. Gard is seen as the proponent of a cadre of vices in a mostly lawless town: saloons, brothels, wood-planked sidewalks and shootouts at noon. Everything stereotypical about the Wild West was evident in Alosta. The very fact that the northern terminuses of its streets didn't line up with the southern ends of Glendora's streets is proof positive that something wicked went on in that town, and Glendora's founders wanted nothing to do with it.

The story of George Whitcomb and the methods and manner associated with his founding of Glendora makes for that much better of a story because of George E. Gard. If it wasn't for the contradictory and conflicting ethics of Gard (namely, that he had a penchant for hard liquor), Glendora's early history would read just like that of any other town in the area. But instead, thanks to the clashing approach to which both men did business, led their lives and built up their individual moralistic foundation, historians today get a glimpse at the greatest struggle to come out of early Glendora history. And almost like a melodramatic vaudevillian silent picture where the audience boos the villain and cheers the hero, we have Whitcomb in one corner, wearing the white hat and leading the good and the righteous, and Gard in the other in his black hat with the saloons and brothels.

It seems that without the sinner, it is difficult to write about the saint, but was Gard the wicked element that doomed Alosta…or just a man with a different set of principles who allowed the events that transpired in Alosta to unfold without his help or hindrance? Well, yes and no.

First, the yes: Gard was looking to make a quick buck on the speculation of land sales around Glendora. He wasn't as honest as Whitcomb in offering quality property for a fair price. Pflueger's *Glendora* puts it well into perspective: "The boom was ridden for all that it was worth…Many business transactions were conducted in the tower of the Hotel Correll. Lots would be pointed out and suckers would sign their names on dotted lines without knowing for sure what they had purchased."

The largest myth surrounding Gard—and the biggest misconception cited as to why Alosta failed as a town—was that Gard quickly left town when the land boom came to an abrupt halt at the end of 1888. Pflueger claimed that "Alosta was a casualty. Whitcomb and his assistants stayed by Glendora, but the promoters of Alosta took their bags full of money and departed." That is absolutely not true. Gard never permanently moved away from Alosta (nor from Gladstone, where he also owned property), at least not until the very end of his life. The only mention of his death is in a 1904 annual publication of the Historical Society of Southern California and the Society of Pioneers of Los Angeles County that notes that he passed on March 10 of that year in Pasadena.

The facts surrounding Gard's life are few and not especially revealing. He was born in 1843 to Dr. William V.H. Gard and Lucretia Williamson, both from prominent Ohio families (he a surgeon and she a teacher). By the time George Gard was six, he was an orphan and was sent to live with his maternal grandfather, Garrett Williamson. When he turned sixteen, he followed his uncle, Henry Williamson, to California. For unknown reasons, Henry was transporting to California a collection of thoroughbred racehorses and a herd of cattle, and while living with his uncle in San Jose, Gard learned to appreciate thoroughbred horses. Later in life, according to the *American Stud Book*, written by Sanders Dewees Bruce in 1889, Gard was the owner of a bay mare, Belmontine. His horse was quite a successful breeder and racer. Between the years 1885 and 1890, she sired Musidora, Grant O, Alosta and Barren.

Gard immediately started work at his uncle's sawmill, Lovejoy & Gard's Saw Mills in San Jose. Two years later, he left his uncle's house and moved out on his own, becoming the assistant superintendent of the Mariposa Mining Company's mills.

During the Civil War, Gard was looking for excitement, so he enlisted in the Union army late in the war. He entered the United States military service in 1864 as first sergeant of Company H, Seventh

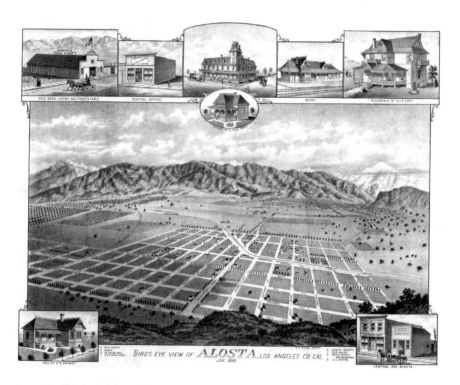

A map by Edwin S. Moore (the same artist who penned Glendora's map) shows the town as George Gard imagined it could be in 1887. With the exception of Colorado, Walnut and Mauna Loa, none of Gard's street names have survived.

California Volunteer Infantry, and he was with that command in Arizona and New Mexico until March 1866, when he was discharged along with his company.

Gard moved to Los Angeles in the early part of 1868 and started the Los Angeles Ice Company, the first of its kind in Los Angeles to deliver ice to the city. Soon he partnered with a man by the name of Mr. Queen to form Queen and Gard Corporation and built an ice storage building on Main Street in downtown Los Angeles. According to the 1889 edition of *An Illustrated History of Los Angeles County*, ice was brought in from the Truckee River by steamer to San Pedro, and by the time the business turned profitable, most of its customers were keeping their perishables cold for the first time.

In 1869, Gard met and married Catherine "Kate" A. Hammel, the older sister of future Los Angeles County sheriff William Hammel. Kate was born in about 1855 in Washington, D.C., to Prussian parents, which makes her roughly fourteen at time she was wed, and in 1870, she gave birth to William Brant, followed up by Georgetta Miles eight years later. Perhaps Gard's relationship with his new brother-in-law convinced him to take an interest in the politics of Los Angeles (at the time Hammel was a deputy officer), and he soon sold his shares in the Queen and Gard Corporation and landed a job in the office of the county clerk. In 1871, he switched to the city marshal's office, where he earned eighty dollars per month as a deputy marshal. Here he met Emil Harris, a rugged lawman who had emigrated from Prussia at the age of fourteen. They would soon become good friends.

The pair worked so well together that the city council appointed them as the city's first detectives in 1873. However, the following year, Gard was out of work—he hadn't been reappointed to his former position—so he found a place as the county's chief deputy recorder, and he stayed in that capacity until 1879. During this time, thanks to Harris's work in capturing notorious California bandit Tiburcio Vasquez (who was eventually hanged for his crimes in 1875), Emil succeeded in becoming the chief of police in 1877, and this helped springboard Gard into this position as well, earning the rank of Los Angeles chief of police on December 12, 1880. When his term was up, he returned to law enforcement again as a deputy sheriff, but in 1884, he was selected as the Republican candidate for the sheriff's office. He was elected with 2,408 votes and served from 1885 to 1886.

During Gard's term as sheriff, the population of the county demanded that a new jail be built, and he oversaw its construction and the transfer of its prisoners to the New High Street Jail near the end of his term. On December 2, 1886, the *Los Angeles Times* reported that "[t]he prisoners were taken up handcuffed two and two…All their old blankets were left behind and they found comfortable new ones. The beds in the jail were also a pleasant surprise. They are flat hammocks of canvas stretched from wall to wall by straps, and apparently very comfortable. The bathtubs and sanitary appliances in the new quarters are admirable."

At this point in Gard's life, he found himself in the Azusa Valley encountering Whitcomb, creating a conflict and resolving to beat him at his own game by starting his own town between Glendora and Gladstone. There's no information regarding his decision to settle in the valley, but perhaps he had traveled through the area frequently during his various duties, and like many people before and after him, the climate and locales suited him. Gard partnered with Sherman Washburn, landowner in Pasadena and treasurer for the defunct Los Angeles and San Gabriel Valley Railroad (the one that sold out to the Santa Fe the year before), and F.M. Underwood to form the Alosta Land and Water Company. Like the newly laid-out town to the north, Gard plotted streets and set out the lots, ready to make a fortune in land speculation. Whether he was at the right place at the right time or had some business acumen is left to conjecture, but he submitted his official map to the county recorder (whom he probably knew personally) exactly one day after Whitcomb, on September 23, 1887.

Calling his town Alosta was probably particularly irksome to Whitcomb, especially considering that the whole area at the time was recognized by the United States Post Office as Alosta and not Glendora. Those sending mail to Whitcomb himself sent it to the Alosta Post Office (with the location being Alosta, California, and not Glendora). And there was nothing Whitcomb could do about it.

The land boom ended in 1888, but what happened to Gard? Close followers of Glendora's history believe that Gard took his fortune and

Henry Harrison Fuller owned much of the land on which Gard would start his town of Alosta in 1887. Fuller's friend, Postmaster General Frank Hatton, approved a post office in 1883 for the area, which Fuller named Alosta after his daughter, Anna Losta Fuller, seen here.

laughed himself all the way to the bank, perhaps the one his partner Washburn owned in Pasadena. But that just isn't so, and by examining a few details, it is quite clear that Gard had every good intention of building a town called Alosta and hopefully further writing his name in the history books of Southern California with this legacy becoming a success. According to the 1889 edition of *An Illustrated History of Los Angeles County*, "In 1886 Mr. Gard purchased forty acres of land at Gladstone and the next year a tract of land at Alosta. Soon after his purchase he commenced active operations in subdividing his lands and inviting the settlement of that section. Early in 1887, he incorporated the Alosta Land and Water Company, and developed water in the Little Dalton Cañon and piped the same to that tract at an expense of about $25,000."

Why would he go to such great lengths to develop water for a town if he had no interest in its success? This, of course, leads to questions regarding his business practices. Why would he flamboyantly and famously swindle people (who would be his neighbors) out of their money for overpriced land?

From the same article:

> *His present home is located about one-half mile east of Gladstone, where he is establishing one of the representative fruit industries of his section, having now* [1889] *fifteen acres of Washington Navel oranges and a large variety of deciduous fruits on his eighty-acre tract at that point. In addition to his home place he has a tract of 107 acres of hill and valley land, one-fourth of a mile south of Alosta, upon which there is a five-acre orange grove and a two-acre orchard of deciduous fruits. He also has lands on Citrus and Broadway avenues in the Gladstone tract, which is well improved and producing deciduous and citrus fruits, besides business and residence property in Alosta, including wood and coal yard, cottages, etc.*

Nobody this entrenched in the land and in the area just gets up and walks away from it. He didn't sell his land at the end of 1888, when the real estate market collapsed, nor did he run away with the profits, abandoning his property. In addition, it is believed that he couldn't have sold it if he wanted to, given how difficult a time some people were having trying to unload their real estate in the post-boom years. So, what do Glendora's historians say happened to Gard after 1890? Well, nothing specifically, as they all claim that he just got up and left, vanishing into the sunset.

Gard didn't leave Alosta to crumble into the weeds, nor did he abandon his property with his bags of ill-gotten gains. Gard spent four years in Alosta after his term at the sheriff's office ended in 1886, which still places him on his property and in his town until 1890. At this time, he was appointed by President Benjamin Harrison to a four-year term as U.S. marshal for the Southern District of California. Quite contrary to him disappearing and fading away, this was a time when Gard's law enforcement career hit a zenith of success and popularity, thanks to two train robbers, Chris Evans and John Sontag.

A celebratory photograph of train robber John Sontag, gunned down by a posse of various lawmen on June 11, 1893, among them U.S. Marshal George Gard (third from the right, wearing a scarf on his head).

Twenty-seven-year-old John Sontag was working for the Southern Pacific Railroad Company in 1887 and was seriously injured in a yard accident that left him without work. He met and befriended forty-two-year-old farmer Chris Evans, a married man and father of two. The pair started a livery business in Modesto, and four months after the grand opening, it burned to the ground. Then Sontag convinced Evans to start a life of crime.

Regardless of the motives, they began robbing trains near Pixley, Goshen and Visalia in Northern California in 1892. In the first three robberies, they made off with nearly $20,000, killed four people and gained the attention of the nation's best detective agency, Pinkerton, whose members quickly caught up with the men near Fresno. After a harrowing gun battle and narrow escape, Wells Fargo detective John Thacker called on his associate, ex–Los Angeles County sheriff and U.S. marshal George E. Gard, to help in the search. Together with Nevada lawman Fred Jackson, private detective Tom Burns and Fresno County deputy sheriff Hiram Rapelje, they began searching for the men solely at night. They ate cold food and used no campfires during their nine months on the trail. However, on June 11, 1893, they surprised the two bandits outside Visalia at a place called Stone Corral. In an article for the *San Francisco Examiner*, Petey Bigelow interviewed Evans and published this firsthand account: "The first intimation I had of danger was a bullet. John and I was walking leisurely down the trail and were just sitting down upon the old manure heap near the cabin. Suddenly there was a report and a bullet flew past Sontag's head. Then we knew we were in for it. It was the worst fight I ever was in."

Just before dark, Evans was struck several times in the arm and face, and Sontag was mortally wounded in the forehead. According to Evans, "He cried, 'My God, Chris, I'm done for this time.'"

Evans was found eight miles away and went to Folsom Prison without his left arm and right eye, ready to serve a life sentence. He was paroled in 1911 after only serving seventeen years and was banished from California forever. He died in 1917 in Oregon. For his participation in the capture of Sontag (Evans was taken by Tulare deputy sheriff Hall), Gard was supposed to receive $5,000, which he would split between his posse, leaving $1,500 for himself. However, this wasn't the end of it, as a heated debate over the reward money went to court and lasted for years. On December 11, 1896, a federal judge found that John Sontag had been arrested by U.S. Marshal Gard and his posse in accordance with the reward terms.

After this action, George Gard took a position as the chief of detectives with the Southern Pacific Railroad, and this took him all over the Southwest. He later opened his own detective agency and settled at his home again, where he continued raising oranges until his death on March 10, 1904.

So was Gard responsible for the decimation of Alosta as a town? Probably not, as the very fact of him being absent from 1892 until 1893 or 1894 during his term as marshal wouldn't be an important enough catalyst to cause the town to fold up. The main reason would most likely be the lack of permanent settlers. Glendora had a score of families already living around Whitcomb's property when he decided to start Glendora, and those families never left. Alosta, on the other hand, didn't

Boasting fifty rooms, the Hotel Correll was built on the southeast corner of Walnut and Central (now Glendora) avenues in 1887 by S.C. Correll for $16,000. It was later known as the Alosta Hotel and then as Hotel Glendora. It was the oldest building in Glendora by the time it was burned down for practice by the county fire department in the 1950s.

have that church and family foundation to begin with, and given the fact that Gard owned so much of the property, it left little room for others to settle around him without buying into his town.

Alosta died just like Spadra and Gladstone, from lack of interest, lack of a community and lack of a permanency felt in places like Lordsburg (later renamed LaVerne), San Dimas, Azusa and, of course, Glendora.

However, the idea of George Edwin Gard stuffing his luggage with loot and escaping on the first outbound train is preposterous. Gard died in Pasadena at a hospital after an illness. His wife, Catherine, however, died almost two dozen years later at the Gard family house in the town of Alosta, which she had never left.

Hayden Jones's Fateful Train Ride of 1911

Much like automobile accidents today, train wrecks were an all-too-common event one hundred years ago; it seems the faster man desires to travel, the more common the accidents. The 1922 *Report of the Railroad Commission of California* lists two rail-related accidents in Glendora. On October 10, 1920, the Los Angeles Division of the Atchison, Topeka and Santa Fe Railway Company reported a "grade crossing" accident that resulted in five fatalities, and six months later, on March 24, 1921, the Southern Division of the Pacific Electric reported one fatality and one injury during an accident along its line at the Grand Avenue crossing. Additionally, on May 4, 1912, Charles Henry Converse (who built the Converse Building downtown) was crossing the Santa Fe tracks at Loraine Avenue in Glendora when he was struck and killed by a fast-approaching train.

But an accident involving two trains on the same track is an unusual event, especially in Glendora's history; one caused quite a commotion on the morning of March 16, 1911.

A head-on collision of two AT&SF locomotives happened at about 10:00 a.m. on that Wednesday morning directly east from the eastern base of the South Hills, opposite where Linfield Street and Deserta Drive dead-end on the eastern side of the Santa Fe right-of-way (off Lone Hill).

On March 16, 1911, an eastbound train collided with a westbound train on the AT&SF tracks just east of the South Hills. There were no injuries, and despite the damage, both locomotives resumed duty months later.

Coming from San Dimas, the Santa Fe tracks turn gradually north toward the South Hills between Bonita and San Dimas Avenue and Lone Hill. They cross what is now the 57 freeway and head northwest until they straighten out just north of what is now the 210 freeway. From here, they point directly north for only about 1,500 feet before making the sharp western turn around the northeast corner of the South Hills to follow Route 66 through Glendora.

This sharp western turn around the South Hills creates a rather large blind spot to any eastbound train. Each train only carried four cars (three passenger cars and a cargo car), so they weren't that long, and the engines could handle the weight. With only about five hundred feet of visibility, neither train would have had enough time to stop had it come completely around the corner to see the second train headed its way.

But what really happened? Hayden Jones, the station agent who was operating one of the locomotives at the time, completely admitted to being entirely at fault for the crash. He is pointed out in the March 15, 1911 edition of the *San Dimas Eagle* as freely admitting "in the most possible manly way that the blame for the wreck lies with him." It seems as though Jones was distraught over the illness of his wife, who had recently had a baby. "Several nights of anxiety over the condition of his wife," the article explains, "incidental to the birth of his first child, may have contributed somewhat to the conditions that lead up to the unfortunate accident."

Incidentally, on that hill alongside Lone Hill Avenue (which is how Lone Hill got its name) is now the Glendora Friends Church (of the Quaker faith). In the distance, there is a stand of tall trees reaching up into the hills to the left. Those line what is now known as San Dimas Canyon Road, but most of those trees are now gone, with a few possible exceptions. The white farmhouse at the far left of the picture here is in the vicinity of what is now the Glendora Country Club, which means that it could very well be the house of Charles C. Warren (as his first house was located on Amelia, just a short distance north of Route 66). The Davenports, Joys and Cunninghams all lived in the area at the time, but Warren undoubtedly had the largest house.

Both of the engines, according to the Whyte system for classifying steam locomotives by wheel arrangement (devised by Frederick Methvan Whyte about 1900), were 4-6-0 locomotives, nicknamed "Ten-Wheelers" because they had four lead wheels, six drive wheels and no trailing wheels. Despite being employed by AT&SF and ending up being attached by the noses, their wheel configuration was all they had in common.

The southbound train (on the left in the image) is AT&SF 481, the 14th locomotive (out of 30) built in the 468 class, constructed at the Rhode Island Locomotive Works in 1900. According to 1906 literature from Baldwin Locomotive Works about the equipment on the AT&SF Railway System:

> *These locomotives had cylinders twenty inches in diameter by twenty-six-inches stroke, the diameter of the driving wheels being sixty-nine inches and the steam pressure 180 pounds; thus giving them a tractive power of 23,000 pounds. The boiler was of the Wagon-Top type, 60*

inches in diameter. It contained 262 tubes, two inches in diameter and 14 feet 3 inches long, the firebox being 102 inches long by 40 and one-quarter inches wide. The grate area was 28 and five-tenths square feet. The total weight was 155,610 pounds, the weight on driving wheels being 120,410 pounds. The tank capacity was 5,000 gallons.

Rhode Island Locomotive Works was located in Providence, Rhode Island, and produced about 3,400 locomotives between 1867 and 1906, when production there was shut down. Five years earlier, in 1901, the works merged with seven other locomotive manufacturers to form the American Locomotive Company (ALCO) in an effort to compete with the then largest manufacturer of locomotives, Baldwin. Strangely enough, after locomotive production ceased in 1906, ALCO began building automobiles and trucks, which were decidedly unpopular and not profitable. The production only lasted seven years until 1913.

The jewel of the accident is the locomotive on the right in the image, the AT&SF 498, the first of five engines in its class and built by the Baldwin Locomotive Works in 1901. It was powered by a four-cylinder Vauclain compound-type boiler, which offered more

Hayden Jones, flanked by what can only be guessed are his superiors, admitted to falling asleep at the throttle when the collision occurred.

efficiency but a higher breakdown rate. Though this engine is generally known as a Baldwin locomotive, it was built during a time when the Baldwin Locomotive Works was doing business as Burnham, Williams and Company, as there was rarely a period in Baldwin's history when it wasn't changing its name. Incidentally, Baldwin has a small connection with Glendora's history. In 1930, controlling interest in George Whitcomb's company, the Whitcomb Locomotive Works, was sold to Baldwin Locomotives Works.

The company was founded in 1831 by Matthias Baldwin, and it operated in a plant on Broad Street in Philadelphia for seventy-one years until moving to Eddystone, Pennsylvania, in 1912. From a 1900 Baldwin catalogue: "Mathias Baldwin built his first steam locomotive in 1832, with the assistance of a railroad mechanic named Andrew Vauclain. Five decades later, his son Samuel M. Vauclain joined the Baldwin Locomotive Works Co. Vauclain developed the compound locomotive in 1889, an achievement that changed the face of the railroad industry."

The concept of a compound locomotive was explained in an article titled "Building of American Locomotives" in the June 7, 1902 issue of *Scientific American*:

> *The two pistons on either side are connected to a common crosshead, and each pair of cylinders is cast in one piece with the piston, steam-chest and one-half of the saddle. The valve, which is double and hollow, controls the steam admission and exhaust of both cylinders. The exhaust steam on the high-pressure cylinder becomes the supply steam for the low-pressure cylinder; and as the steam for the high-pressure cylinder enters the steam-chest at both ends the valve is in practically perfect balance. A by-pass valve is provided to admit live steam to the low-pressure cylinder in starting.*

Essentially, the steam is compressed and used twice to turn the pistons, once under high pressure and a second time under lower pressure, making for a very efficient running engine.

As for the accident, it was a surprise when nobody was seriously hurt, and seeing how the tenders on both trains were pancaked into the cabs

Passengers from the train and spectators from nearby Glendora and San Dimas communities watch as AT&SF cranes clear the tracks.

of the engines, it must have been a close scrape for Hayden Jones and his counterpart in the other engine. The crowds surrounding the wrecked locomotives are mostly passengers from both trains out to inspect the damage and relive the experience with other passengers (and to grab a souvenir or two), but the incident was enough to draw attention from locals who came out to see the spectacle.

Both trains survived to run the rails again. Soon after the accident in 1911, the "compound locomotive," the 498, was stripped of its extra abilities and spent the rest of its days as a single boiler until it was scrapped in 1929. The 481 on the right was repaired and remained in service until 1938.

As for Hayden Jones, he returned to work and to his growing family. Jones became the choir director for the Union Church in San Dimas and held that post for more than thirty years.

The Story of Old Baldy

One of the most historically omnipresent symbols of the harshness of settling the Azusa Valley in the nineteenth century is also the largest and oldest. Standing tall above not only what would become Glendora but also the entire San Gabriel mountain range and the eastern high deserts is Mount San Antonio, soaring into the sky 10,064 feet above sea level.

Mount San Antonio marks a boundary between San Bernardino and Los Angeles Counties and enjoys the distinction of having two summits, with a difference of only a mere seventy-six feet. These two summits give the perception that the mountain has a wide, rounded top, which led to the creation of its better-known nickname, Mount Baldy (or Old Baldy), a moniker earned during the Wheeler survey in 1878 via local miners who felt that the barren top of the mountain resembled a balding man's head due to its lack of trees and generally gray appearance.

The first people to see the mountain and traverse its snowcapped peaks were more than likely the Serrano Indians, one of half a dozen Indian communities that lived in the mountain's shadows. A main cross-mountain Indian trail passed near what is now known as "Baldy Notch," which connected the Los Angeles Basin with the desert. This later became the "Old Baldy Wagon Trail," which was widened into a road by Los Angeles County in 1930.

Invariably, it is not surprising that the local Indians would give a name to the largest feature in the area. The Serranos knew it by any number of names, such as Jóaka'j, Juáka, Joakaits and Hesakkopa; the Gabrielinos called it Juáka'j and Hifá'do and also referred to it as Yoát, which means snow; the Luiseños knew it as Hifá'doyah; the Cauhillas called it Hifá'doga; and the Mohaves named it Avii Kwatiinyam.

According to an article published by the Sierra Club, "A Serrano Indian legend survives that tells of the arrival of their ancestors upon this peak from somewhere to the North—they followed the pure white eagle of their Land God, who perched on this summit, whereupon they settled here. It was a place where Mountain Sheep were hunted, and this would definitely give it a sacred connotation since these animals were held in considerable reverence."

As with many Native American place names, all of the various titles given to Mount San Antonio were soon erased when the Europeans visited. The one name that eventually stuck was proclaimed by Antonio Maria Lugo on June 13, 1841, the feast day for Saint Anthony of Padua.

A photograph of Mount Baldy in all its splendor, taken by James Walter Collinge in 1913. As a photographer of the early 1900s, Collinge's work was extensively exhibited at both national and international shows and exemplified the romantic images of the pictorialism movement in America during the era.

Six hundred years after Saint Anthony's death, in 1841, at the height of his own power in the Los Angeles area, Antonio Maria Lugo christened the tallest mountain he had ever seen Mount San Antonio after Saint Anthony of Padua. The inspiration is quite clear: Antonio Lugo was born sometime about 1776 at the Mission San Antonio de Padua in Monterey and was given his name by Father Junipero Serra himself.

Because he enjoyed a closeness with his namesake and the heritage of the mission, Lugo named many things after the saint, including his property Rancho San Antonio. This extensive tract of land was given to him in 1810 as a Spanish land grant because of his extensive service in the military. He added in 1841 Rancho Santa Ana, encompassing a total of 29,513 acres, including many of the cities of east Los Angeles and portions well into Orange County toward the current city of Santa Ana.

According to Dr. Roy Whitehead in his book *Lugo*:

> *Don Antonio Maria Lugo rode around Los Angeles and his Rancho San Antonio in great splendor. He never adopted American dress, culture or language and still spoke only Spanish. He rode magnificent horses, sitting in his $1,500 silver trimmed saddle erect and stately, with his sword strapped to the saddle beneath his left leg. People knew him far and wide, and even the Indians sometimes named their children after him, as he was one Spanish Don that they admired.*

Lugo later became the mayor of Los Angeles in 1816 and 1818 and a judge in 1833–34, and he held a position on the city council in 1837–38. When California became part of the United States in 1850, Lugo, as did most holders of Spanish and Mexican land grants, began losing portions of his land to the growing population of Americans. Lugo died in 1860, but the ranch adobe on his Rancho San Antonio property, however, continued to be used by the Lugo family and still survives to this day.

The first printed reference to the mountain being called Mount San Antonio is found in an 1858 edition of *Los Angeles Southern Vineyard*, published by Jonathan Trumbull Warner (aka Don Juan J. Warner), but the first known ascent wasn't accomplished until 1878, achieved by Louis Nell, a member of the famous Wheeler survey that had been supervised by West Point graduate First Lieutenant (later Captain) George Montague Wheeler.

In 1872, Congress authorized a plan to map the portion of the United States west of the one hundredth meridian at a scale of eight miles to the inch, with its main goal being to make topographic maps of the southwestern United States, but according to the University of Nevada's website, "In addition he was to ascertain everything related to the physical features of the region; discover the numbers, habits, and disposition of Indians in the section; select sites for future military installations; determine facilities available for making rail or common roads; and note mineral resources, climate, geology, vegetation, water sources, and agricultural potential." The official surveys lasted until 1879, when his work was collected together with that of Clarence King and John Wesley Powell and reorganized to become the United States Geological Survey.

How exactly it was decided that Louis Nell was to be the first to the top of the mountain isn't known, but it is recorded that the survey team made the summit via Lytle Creek and calculated the elevation of the top as 10,191 feet, only 127 feet off the current reading. In a *New York Times* article from September 13, 1876, Nell was listed as the lead topographer for the Colorado portion of the project (which included New Mexico), headed by Lieutenant Eric Sergland from the Army Corps of Engineers. While the article points out that Wheeler himself was in charge of the California contingent, perhaps two years later Nell was given a portion of Southern California. The *New York Times* article comments on camp life:

> *The organizing camp of the California section is here, as I have stated, in a meadow on the outskirts of growing Carson City. The ground is littered with boxes containing stores, instruments, and other parts of equipment. The topographers are testing and adjusting their instruments; the packers are fitting the apparajoes, or pack saddles, to the mules; the odometer recorders are out on the road correcting their instruments by a chain-measured mile, and the meteorologists are in a corner by themselves with their barometers and wet and dry bulb thermometers.*

About this time, at least as it was reported in an 1871 edition of the *Los Angeles Star*, people started to refer to Mount San Antonio as Mount Baldy and Old Baldy. Though credit is given to the miners who had flocked to the mountain in 1869 after gold was discovered just below Baldy Notch by F.L. Richie, it is not known if any of the gold diggers (and, later, hydraulic miners) ever climbed to the top.

The first person on record to make the ascent to the top of Old Baldy for the purpose of economic gain was William B. Dewey in 1882 (he went on to climb the mountain an astonishing 133 times). He found the area overrun with deer, bighorn sheep, grizzly bear and mountain lion; and he was later a guide for a very popular vacation spot called Stoddard's Resort before opening his own place in 1910, Angel's Camp (later called Baldy Summit Inn), only eighty feet from the top. It included two small stone buildings and several tents—a small village that guests could access by riding horses up from what was then called Camp Baldy. High winds were a constant threat to Dewey and his camp, but ultimately a fire extinguished his hopes in 1912, and he never rebuilt.

However, the popularity of the mountain became infectious. Charles Francis Saunders in his *Southern Sierras of California* (1923) observed that "[i]f you have anything of the Californian in you, you mark [Mount San Antonio] for the objective of an outing sometime." Perhaps because of this advice, Baldy had become the most climbed mountain in Southern California by the 1920s.

Thanks to Dewey and Stoddard and the increased popularity of outdoor sports and healthy living, Mount Baldy was heralded as the first major ski resort, and in 1922, USC professor George O. Bauwens first ascended the mountain on skis, looking for better access to the slopes in the wintertime. Bauwens later helped found the Sierra Club Ski Mountaineers in 1935. From Bob Brinton's 1945 *Encyclimpedia Brintonica*: "During the spring of 1935, the enthusiasms of the small group were enhanced considerably by the entrance of George Bauwens into the fold. George, a pioneer in ski mountaineering first in the German Alps and later in Southern California, saw the need for a system of ski lodges and had the ability to plan and build the shelters."

Sunshine and snow juxtapose in this very popular image of Mount Baldy, showing the ease of citrus production against snowy twin peaks of the tallest mountain in Los Angeles County.

Access for hikers was further eased when Bear Flats Trail and the Devil's Backbone Trail were reworked and made safer (they were originally created in the 1890s), and the first commercial ski lift wasn't put into operation until 1952 in the Baldy Notch area.

However, the name Mount San Antonio has had its share of difficulties in sticking to modern maps. San Antonio Mountain was listed as its name on a 1931 USGS map; Baldy and Old Baldy are found on a 1943 San Bernardino map; Old Baldy Peak showed up on the Army Mapping Service in 1952; San Antonia Peak was used by Rand McNally; and even the name Supreme Summit of the Sierra Madre was given by Drury in 1935.

Even the U.S. Post Office was given the run around when it came to various place names on the mountain. From *California's Geographic Names: A Gazetteer of Historic and Modern Names* by David L. Durham (1998): "Postal authorities established Camp Baldy post office in 1913, changed the name to Mt. Baldy in July 1, 1951 (by petition of the residents), changed it to Mount Baldy in 1966, and changed it back to Mt. Baldy in 1975."

The history of Baldy Village starts with Charles R. Baynham buying the property in 1906 and calling it Camp Baynham; F.W. Palmer purchased the place in 1910 and changed the name to Camp Baldy. Ann Courtney and Fred Courtney opened Bear Canyon resort just below Camp Baldy in 1921, and R.D. Shiffer started a resort called Eleven Oaks next to Bear Canyon Resort the same year. The community of Mount Baldy is known locally as Baldy Village.

Mount San Antonio isn't without its small claim to international fame, at least fame in the scientific community, as the site of the then best calculation of the speed of light, made by William Bowie, the chief of Division of Geodesy of the U.S. Coast and Geodetic Survey in the 1920s. It is described in Allan Sandage, Louis Brown and Patricia Parratt Craig's 2004 book, *Centennial History of the Carnegie Institution of Washington*: "In each experiment, a rotating octagon mirror was used to measure the flight time, corrected to vacuum, in the round trip between the two stations. A sightline distance of 22 miles (35km) separated the station on Mount Wilson from a station on Mount San Antonio to the east, known locally as Mount Baldy."

Bowie stated his conclusion that he had "determined the length of this line with greater accuracy than any other line of triangulation in this or any other country." Bowie's distance between the two stations was 35,358.53 meters, or 21.99 miles. His stated accuracy for that distance corresponds to an error of only 0.52 millimeters over 22.00 miles.

Bowie and his geodetic crew used the standard methods of triangulation from base lines whose lengths were determined by special tempered-steel measuring tapes. To achieve a stated accuracy, Bowie's team had to understand the tapes' stretch-under-tension in varying temperature conditions to an accuracy never before attained. The base line from which their triangles originated was a straight horizontal path from Pasadena to the base of Mount San Antonio along the talus slopes of the San Gabriel Mountains. That path—now a major commuter artery through the San Gabriel Valley—is today known as Base Line Road.

In Stanley Wood's 1889 book *Over the Range to the Golden Gate*, he wrote of the magnificence of Mount San Antonio:

> *These majestic snow-capped peaks, towering above their fellows and glistening in the brilliant sunlight, afford a pleasing contrast to the luxuriant semi-tropical growth of the cultivated valley. Here on the upper slope of Ontario we find Orange Groves breathing their delightful fragrance upon the balmy air, free from any suggestion of cold and beyond the reach of blighting frosts, whilst eight or nine miles away the eternal snows keep their silent vigil. Nowhere, probably, on the face of the Globe are Winter and Summer brought into such close juxtaposition. Perpetual summer and eternal winter clasping hands across San Antonio Canon! The spectacle is an extraordinary one, and the more it is considered the more wonderful it becomes.*

Sally Rand of Glendora

The Chicago World's Fair, held in 1933 and 1934, was billed as "A Century of Progress," a slogan dedicated to the 100th anniversary of the city of Chicago. It spotlighted the industrial, scientific and social achievements up to that time. Staged on 424 acres on the waters of Lake Michigan between Twelfth and Thirty-ninth Streets, it was unlike any fair before it, drawing more than 48 million visitors in the two years it ran, which was a significant percentage of the 122 million people living in America at the time. It opened on Saturday, May 27, 1933, and Sally Rand was in Chicago looking for a break, a hand up in her stalled career. Not being a person to stand idly by waiting for something to happen, she was well prepared to make an impression, force a turning point in her dreams of success. What followed would catapult her to fame and fortune and turn her into a household name.

Sally Rand was born Helen Gould Beck (though the name on her Social Security card is Harriet Helen Beck) on January 2, 1904, in the small village of Elkton in Hickory County, Missouri, about 150 miles southeast of Kansas City. Her father was a West Point graduate and army colonel, and her mother, Annette Mary Grove, was a schoolteacher and a writer for various local newspapers; while she was still in elementary school, the Beck family moved to Jackson County,

Born Helen Gould Beck, Sally Rand became a household name in the 1930s, parlaying that fame throughout her lifetime.

Missouri, to a suburb east of Kansas City. There Helen Gould Beck took an interest in show business.

At the age of six, she saw famous Russian ballerina Anna Pavlova dance, and she convinced her parents to pay for ballet lessons. Seven years later, while still attending Central High School, she worked in a German beer garden and danced as a chorus girl in vaudeville performances at the Empress Theater in Kansas City, catching the eye of the drama critic Goodman Ace of the *Kansas City Journal*.

Taking the stage name Billie Beck, she found work in Chicago with Adolph Bohm's Chicago Ballet Company, and she also studied modeling at the Art Institute. Partly because of Goody's praise for young Beck, she was "discovered" by Gus Edwards, a popular singer, actor and owner of a successful vaudeville company, the Gus Edwards Music Hall in New York. Edwards suggested that she move to Hollywood. In 1923, she was a mild success as one of Mack Sennett's bathing beauties. Sennett is, of course, famous for starting the Keystone Studios in then Edendale, California (now part of Echo Park), the first totally enclosed sound stage and studio in Hollywood history. Many famous people got their start there, including Charlie Chaplin, Bing Crosby, W.C. Fields and, naturally, the Keystone Kops.

From Sennett, Beck was cast in bit roles in several silent pictures by Cecil B. DeMille, playing in ten movies using the name Beck, starting with *The Dressmaker from Paris* in 1925. DeMille, famous for changing the names of his players, did the same for Helen Beck, and as the legend goes, he was looking at a Rand McNally "Auto Chum" Atlas at the time he picked her name. When he cast her as the slave girl to Mary Magdalene in *King of Kings*, she was from then on known as Sally Rand (ironically, her name didn't make the final credits).

In the three years since her arrival in Hollywood, she had been in nineteen pictures, but with the advent of sound, pointedly with the popularity and success of the 1927 "talkie" *The Jazz Singer*, the industry changed, switching over to focus on actors who not only looked good but also had a voice that matched.

In 1927, she was encouraged by the news that she was one of twelve other girls to be chosen as a WAMPAS Baby Star, a promotional campaign sponsored by the Western Association of Motion Picture Advertisers. The group chose thirteen women each year whom it believed to be on the threshold of stardom, and the women were given extensive media coverage. The chosen thirteen were formally introduced at a coming-out party, known as the WAMPAS Frolic, an event covered by the media much like today's Academy Award ceremonies.

Meanwhile, the promise of future success in film was beginning to fade. Sally Rand's Ozark twang and a noticeable lisp were too much of an obstacle to continue working. *The Black Feather* was Rand's last silent picture, and she wasn't able to find work again until 1932, when she landed the bit role as "Crocodiles' Victim" in DeMille's *Sign of the Cross*, a Roman love story.

For the next few years, work was difficult to come by. In *Striptease: The Untold History of the Girlie Show* (2004), Rachel Shteir explained Rand's post–silent film situation:

Exiled from Hollywood in the late twenties, Rand dabbled in vaudeville and for a time traveled on the Orpheum circuit with an act called Sally and Her Boys. After the stock market crashed, she found herself adrift. She worked briefly in New York and arrived in Chicago in the touring burlesque show, "Sweethearts on Parade." Soon, she was out of work completely, almost 30 years old and stuck back in Chicago again, months before the Fair was set to open.

In the early 1930s, groups like New York's Society for the Suppression of Vice and New England's Watch and Ward Society were putting pressure on local officials to close down burlesque shows and strip clubs on the grounds of strengthening the moral fiber of their respective cities. In 1933, newly appointed Supreme Court justice John O'Brien, intent on distinguishing himself as a strong reformer, declared, "Hereafter there will never be tolerated the removal of clothes on any stage in New York City in an indecent manner." As a result, exotic dancers, burlesque performers and run-of-the-mill strippers flocked to Chicago, a town then seemingly loose on morals, an image repackaged as "culturally progressive." Mae West, Francis Parks and Faith Bacon, among many others, were soon packing the houses with crowds of people wishing to escape the reality of the Depression, if only for one night of comedy and beautiful women.

Rand soon landed a job at the Paramount Club at 16 East Huron in downtown Chicago, an Eighteenth-Amendment-be-damned speakeasy on the affluent Gold Coast with a patron list that included one of Al Capone's henchmen, Machine Gun Jack McGurn. Here at the Paramount Club, Sally Rand first did her fan dance to a very disinterested audience.

Rand wasn't the first to use fans as part of a dance number, and although it is relatively impossible to pin it on one performer—especially considering that the origins of the fan dance lie in Korean cultural dances of the 1500s, centuries-old Japanese performances and several subcategories of contemporary Spanish flamenco dancing—it was generally accepted (by everyone except Rand, that is) that the first to bring the fan dance to the stages of America was Faith Bacon, a twenty-year-old Broadway dancer at Ed Carroll's "Vanities of 1930."

Meanwhile, back in Chicago in 1933, Rand was looking for ways of advancing her career, of marketing herself and of gaining publicity, and the Chicago Fair was her ticket. She was an acquaintance of Charlie Weber, the county commissioner who owned the concessions at the Streets of Paris, and after repeatedly asking to do her fan dance at one of his shows, he continually turned her down. Her frustration grew. Years later, she shared in an interview with Studs Terkel, exclaiming, "The Streets of Paris was sponsored by the high and mighty of this town."

This gave birth to an idea. It involved a white horse, a Lady Godiva "outfit," Mrs. William Randolph Hearst and the Beaux Arts Ball at the Congress Hotel the night before the exposition was to premiere. Whether

Sally Rand made her break in show business with a publicity stunt on the eve of the Chicago World's Fair in 1933 by dressing up as Lady Godiva and crashing Mrs. William Randolph Hearst's Beaux Arts Ball at the Congress Hotel the night before the exposition was to premiere. The next day, she got a job at the "Streets of Paris."

Sally Rand was actually interested in cultivating a cultural argument against the vast ocean of difference that separated the rich from the poor in Depression-era Chicago, she ultimately decided to crash the Beaux Arts Ball as a protest to the lavishness of the city's upper crust. "There were bread lines, and people were starving," she recalled, "yet women in Chicago had the bad taste to have themselves photographed in gowns they were going to wear at the Ball. One was made of thousand-dollar bills…it was such in bad taste."

According to *World of Fairs: The Century-of-Progress Expositions* by Robert W. Rydell (1993):

> *The night before the fair opened, with the preview party in full swing, Rand brought her Lady Godiva act to the fair. Because no motorized vehicles were allowed on the fairgrounds, she unloaded her horse onto a boat. The rest, as she later explained, became history: "At the yacht landing of The Streets of Paris, there was a little Frenchman who spoke no English. He figured that a broad that arrives in a boat with a horse is supposed to be there. So he opened the gate. The master of ceremonies, poor soul, figured: God, here's a woman with a horse and nobody told me about it…the fanfare sounded and the MC announced: Now, Lady Godiva will take her famous ride. Music played. Every photographer in the business, especially the Hearst ones, were there."*

The next day, May 27, Sand Rand got the job, and because of her, the Streets of Paris was one of the only (if not the only) shows to make a profit in Chicago.

But what did the fan dance look like? According to Shteir's *Striptease* book, in part quoting Rand herself:

> *"I attempt to prove the Rand is quicker than the eye," she quipped. Wearing a peroxide blonde wig, naked (or mostly naked) under a blue light, behind two pink ostrich feathers, Rand undulated to Claude Debussy's "Clair de Lune" and a Chopin waltz. "It is just my interpretation of a white bird flying in the moonlight at dusk," she said. "A white bird flying up. It flies up to the moonlight. It is dusk.*

It flies low. It flutters. Then it begins to climb into the moonlight. Finally it rests." The writers Frederick Lewis Allen depicted her as a media event: *"The crowds surged to see her coming down the velvet covered steps with her waving fans (and apparently little else) before both she and Chicago profited."*

Of course, by July 1933, Rand was on trial for indecency charges, and her arrest and trial gained her so much notoriety that she was the subject of water cooler jokes, for example: "Calling all cars, calling all cars, be on the lookout for Sally Rand with a hat on. That is all!" Before the judge, she claimed that if she wore clothes while she danced, the fans would stick to them, making her act more difficult. Her guilty charge was eventually overturned by Superior Court judge Joseph David, who declared, "Some people try to put pants on a horse," adding in Latin, *Honi soit qui mal y pense*, which roughly translates to mean that those who saw obscenity in Rand's act were themselves obscene.

Four arrests in one day at the fair (so it has been said) wasn't going to be the end for Sally Rand in her life, as she was charged again for similar offences to decency and ended up spending ten days in jail and faced $200 in fines. She appealed, incensed that Machine Gun McGurn, who was facing his own trial at roughly the same time, was handed down a sentence half of what hers was, and her sentence was eventually cleared. In the end, she was ordered to wear more clothes, and she decided to call it quits, leaving the Fair for New York.

She swept the country with the popularity of her fan dance and, a year later, developed the bubble dance. In Lisa Krissoff Boehm's 2004 book *Popular Culture and the Enduring Myth of Chicago, 1871–1968*, she asserted that "Sally Rand and her white feather fans were ultimately remembered as symbolic of the 1933 fair. And while few remember 'A Century of Progress' today, the image of the fan dancer still remains. With her success at the fair (she at times grossed in the neighborhood of $5000 a week), Rand launched a dancing career." As Robert Rydell related in his 1993 book *World of Fairs*, "A large ostrich fan used in an exhibit in the New York World's Fair of 1939 was declared, 'The Symbol of the Chicago Fair.'"

Sally Rand proved that sex sells, setting up burlesque shows from New York to San Francisco. Shown here is an advertisement postcard for "Sally Rand's Dude Ranch" at Amon Carter's Fort Worth Frontier Centennial Exposition. The show was rechristened "Sally Rand's Nude Ranch" for San Francisco's Golden Gate International Exposition.

For the rest of her life, she had basically only two acts, the fan dance and the bubble dance, which she performed in a variety of venues, from "Sally Rand's Dude Ranch" at Amon Carter's Fort Worth Frontier Centennial Exposition and the rechristened "Sally Rand's Nude Ranch" at San Francisco's Golden Gate International Exposition to local Rotary meetings, clubs, state fairs and county fairs.

From the 2002 book *San Francisco: True Stories* by James O'Reilly, Larry Habegger and Sean O'Reilly:

> *Jerry Bundsen worked as a Press Agent for Sally Rand and her Nude Ranch. He remembers Sally Rand "as being all business. She had her girls all decked out with western outfits without tops and with skimpy bottoms. Sally would get up on the balcony where the patrons couldn't*

see her or hear her and she'd yell to the girls: 'Come on Nadine. Get over there and jump more, will you? And Helen, for God's sake, get up off your duff and walk over and bend down to pick the basketballs up.' She used to stand there like a maestro running an orchestra."

With her wealth and fame expanding as each year progressed, her popularity caused Hollywood to once again beckon her return. She starred opposite George Raft and Carole Lombard in Wesley Ruggles's *Bolero* and later went on to star as the lead in a movie called *The Sunset Murder Case* in 1938. It was originally named *The Sunset Strip Case*, but censors found it too much of a double meaning between the street name and the fact that Sally Rand was the star. It was banned in several cities, and lawsuits around the country attempted to keep the movie from being shown. As a result of this and the bankruptcy of the studio Grand National and its president, E.W. Hammons, the movie wasn't released officially until 1941.

Meanwhile, it is purported that sometime before her Chicago fan dance debut, she ended up in Glendora, California, and it is only speculation as to why. More than likely, it was during her silent film era of the 1920s, while she was in Hollywood. In the 1980s, columnist Bobbie Battler wrote an article for the *Glendora Press* about the Jonathan Duncan Ranch (on the corner of Loraine and Leadora). She reported that Ella Kisling Duncan (wife of Jonathan) was related to Ernest and "Mary Annette" Kisling, whom Battler claimed is the mother and stepfather of the "famous Sally Rand." That would be a good reason to visit relatives in Glendora in the 1920s, as she probably knew very few people in Southern California, and the timing is right: the Duncans sold the property to L.D. Stith by 1936, when Rand was in New York and Fort Worth.

Toward the end of her life, in the 1970s, Sally Rand owned the quaint little bungalow at 325 North Glendora Avenue, which could very well have been her house the whole time she claimed Glendora as her hometown. In her obituary in the September 1, 1979 edition of the *New York Times*, it notes of her life in Glendora: "When her son entered school, she became active in the Glendora, Calif., Parent Teacher Association and continued her civic activities." In the early 1950s, a

Built on the corner of Sierra Madre and Valley Center, the "Sally Rand House" was designed and built for publicity purposes by Foster Rhodes Jackson, a one-time student of Frank Lloyd Wright.

house was built on the corner of Sierra Madre and Valley Center as a promotional venture for an ultramodern housing design called the "Sally Rand House."

The house, designed by Foster Rhodes Jackson, a one-time student of Frank Lloyd Wright, was dismantled and relocated to a home show in Los Angeles and then reassembled on the grounds again. Whether or not Rand actually owned the house or the land is up for questioning, but the house didn't last long. By the 1960s, it was gone.

A *Miami Herald* article by Don Ediger from August 20, 1967, sums up most of her career:

> *By 1935 she was drawing 1,800 persons a night at the old Merry-Go-Round at Biscayne and 86th St. [Miami] A few years later she danced in The Miami Herald parking lot. Of course, at that time it was the Frolics Club. Later, she was a frequent star at Palm Island's Latin Quarter and the Olympia for $2,500 a week. In 1944, Sally*

turned up at a bond rally not far from the Grove Playhouse and visited the Naval Hospital in Key West. She bought a house in Key West, lived there a while and adopted a son, Sean Orion. Arrested in 1946 in California, she danced for the judge in the courtroom and was acquitted. Tax officials closed in on her. She lost her home in Key West to the federal government. Two marriages failed. The year 1950 found her talking before Lions Clubs and Jaycees.

When she was fifty-two years old, she went back to college to finish her degree (she had taken some courses at Christian College in Columbia, Missouri, now known as Columbia College), and she later put that degree to good use as a speech therapist in Pomona, a "career" that she may have had a personal devotion to due to her lisp and her accent. During her time in school, she said that she found God in a mathematics college textbook, and from then on, she devoted a great deal of her time to the church and various civic organizations in Glendora. She was good friends with the Rubels and gave speeches at the Woman's Club and at Kiwanis meetings in the 1970s.

She herself admitted that she worked forty weeks a year until roughly 1973, performing her routine an estimated fifty thousand times. For Rand, there was a final grand tour in the 1970s.

After a 1974 performance in Los Angeles (one of her last), entertainment critic Sue Cameron wrote of her performance: "The way she moves those fans is an art. Her special campaign today is 'the value of senior citizens,' and in the cities where she plays she often addresses local Kiwanis Clubs on the topic. 'I'm not the type to sit on the porch and watch life go by,' she says, and given the choice, she thinks most other senior citizens would not be either."

At Christmastime 1975, she interrupted a $1,500-a-week booking in Seattle to fly to Glendora, where she prepared a "huge crown-roast Christmas dinner" for members of her church and spent the holidays with her family. Then, flying off again on her appointed rounds, she laughed, "What in heaven's name is strange about a grandmother dancing nude? I'll bet lots of grandmothers do it."

Sally Rand finished up her career where it had really begun, Chicago. In November 1978, she performed for the last time. The *Chicago Tribune* reviewed her performance and complimented her seventy-four-year-old body: "Her figure is attractive too. Her waist is slim, her bosom full. Sally explains that easily: 'Those fans weigh seven and a half pounds apiece. You wave them around for 42 years and you're going to develop pectoral muscles that will hold your boobs up very effectively.' Rand said that she 'has new fans but the same fanny.'"

Regardless, in early August 1979, news accounts noted that she was seriously ill, but in an interview when she was seventy-two years old, Rand was quoted as saying, "God knows I like doing this. It's better than doing needlepoint on the patio."

Toward the end of Ediger's 1967 *Miami Herald* article, he asked Rand about her son, Sean, being the most important person in her life. "I picked him up after a ball game this spring and overheard him talking with two friends. One of them asked, 'What's it like to have Sally Rand as a mother?' Sean said he liked it, but his other friend paused a minute and then said very slowly, 'Who is Sally Rand?'"

Sally Rand died at the Foothill Presbyterian Hospital in Glendora of congestive heart failure on August 31, 1979, at the age seventy-five. A simple stone marks her grave at the Oakdale Memorial Cemetery on Grand Avenue.

She summed up her own life with just a hint of regret: "I have been successful, and I am grateful for my success. I have had some experiences that I wish I never had had, but that would be true in any business. I cannot say sincerely that I would have chosen just this road to fortune. Perhaps I might have wished for another way. But I took the opportunity that came to me."

Glendora's Auto Camp
and Route 66

For the introduction of *Route 66: Traveler's Guide and Roadside Companion* by Tom Snyder, Bobby Troup tells the story behind his iconic song "(Get Your Kicks on) Route 66," which he wrote on his way to California:

Before World War II, my song, "Daddy," was topping all the charts [Sammy Kaye took "Daddy" to number one in 1941]. *In celebration, I bought this olive-green Buick convertible for myself…and it was in that car that my first wife Cynthia and I started for California.*

The first day we stopped at a Howard Johnson's near Pittsburgh. That was when Cynthia first suggested, quite hesitantly really, that I write a song about US 40. But there didn't seem to be any point because we were going to pick up US 66 soon. Cynthia laughed and said, "Get your kicks on Route 66!" The phrase was so great that I began working on the song right away.

By the time we reached Chicago, I had half the song written. "Route 66" turned out to be one of the best songs I've written, though I didn't realize it at the time.

Before Route 66 became a household name, going west was a tangible mark of progression, one of those inalienable rights outlined within the

Shown here in 1921, Glendora's Auto Camp followed in the footsteps of a popular trend toward vacation via the automobile. The Auto Camp was located on the east side of Michigan Avenue just north of the Dalton Wash.

concept of Manifest Destiny, and the allure of California has been a theme in this country's history for almost two centuries. Glendora, specifically the citrus industry that supported the town's economy for so many decades, directly benefited from the wave of eastern and midwestern immigrants.

The Lincoln Highway was perhaps the first main road to connect the two coasts, stretching from New York to San Francisco, and its direct impact on Los Angeles and the southwest United States was limited. According to the 1919 edition of the *Encyclopedia Americana*, "The Lincoln Highway starts at Times Square, 42d street and Broadway, New York... and the terminus is at Lincoln Park overlooking the Golden Gate." However, most travelers didn't turn left when they arrived at the city by the bay; instead they took up residence in many places in Northern California. Only the determined continued south.

Other roads and highways leading to the Golden State would follow, but none was more popular in myth and folklore than U.S. Route 66. In its original form, Route 66 started at the corner of Jackson and Michigan Avenues in Chicago, Illinois, and didn't end until the intersection of Olympic Boulevard and Lincoln Boulevard in California some 2,450 miles later (contrary to popular belief, it never went as far as the Santa Monica Pier). It was a highway spawned by the demands of a rapidly changing America.

Contrasted with the Lincoln, the Dixie and other highways of its day, Route 66 did not follow a traditionally linear course. Its diagonal course linked hundreds of rural communities in Illinois, Missouri and Kansas to Chicago, thus enabling farmers to transport grain and produce for redistribution. The diagonal configuration of Route 66 was particularly significant to the trucking industry, which by 1930 had come to rival the railroad for preeminence in the American shipping industry. The "Mother Road" (so christened by John Steinbeck in his novel *Grapes of Wrath*) between Chicago and the Pacific Coast traversed essentially flat prairie lands and enjoyed a more temperate climate than northern highways, which made it especially appealing to truckers.

From Chicago, Route 66 began as nothing more than a series of intertwining trails headed west, mostly a cobbling together of farm-to-market roads, driveways, paths, old wagon trails, small and rudely improved thoroughfares and downtown streets—as long as it pointed westward and got you out of town and toward the next, it was part of what would be called Route 66. More importantly, it ferried people to California.

Glendorans were excited at the prospect that something so great as a single highway that stretched across the nation would come through their town, and Foothill was suggested as the route through Glendora. After much debate on the subject, it was decided that offering Alosta Avenue to the Mother Road would be a wiser choice, eliminating hoards of traffic that would inevitably follow. In fact, some maps of Route 66 mistakenly list Foothill Boulevard as the link to Route 66, suggesting that you leave Alosta in San Dimas, turn right on Lone Hill and left on Foothill until you reach Citrus Avenue. Without question, this was not true. Alosta has always been on U.S. Route 66.

Until roughly 1926 (though official U.S. Route 66 signs didn't appear until the following year), travelers would have to brave unmarked roads and meandering byways with trepidation that the next town would be just over the horizon. The road was rough and unforgiving, but the promise of California was a tempting motive, and as more cars became a prevalent part of American culture, more people took to the road.

From a 1922 report for the Department of Interior from the National Parks Service, it is clear that the automobile had really mobilized a nation:

> *Undoubtedly the principal factor in the travel movement in this country to-day is the enlarged use of the automobile. It is true the automobile affords a wide freedom in movement of parties limited only by the capacity of the cars, and permits stops at or excursions from any points en route to a particular destination that appeal to the members of the party. It meets the opportunities for out-of-door recreation that we Americans as a sightseeing nation seem to crave, and has come to be considered by many to be the ideal means of vacation travel.*

But once they ended up by the shores of the Pacific, where did they stay? The motel hadn't yet been "invented," and usually a hotel didn't fit in the budget of early travelers. The Department of Interior report from 1922 explains:

> *The great majority of the park visitors now come by motor cars and use the public camping grounds. So extensive has cross-country motor traffic become that practically all cities and towns have established municipal camps and rest grounds for the accommodation of the automobile tourist. Particularly in the West, where the transcontinental traveler is most frequently encountered, facilities approaching in comfort almost the luxurious have been installed in the public camps—electric grills and laundries, baths, and community houses. It is to the automobile that we are indebted more than anything else in the line of transportation for helping Americans feel better acquainted with their own country, and, as our travel figures show, the matchless splendors of the national parks constitute the supreme scenic travel magnets of our country.*

Such an auto camp was available to travelers in Glendora as early as 1921. It was located in an empty field just north of the Dalton Wash on the east side of Michigan Avenue, where the former Neufeld's Promenade was located. According to *Municipal Auto Camps* by Willis Osborne, "It was free and provided visitors with ovens, stove, and a covered kitchen and dining room," and the February 25, 1921 headline for the *Glendora Gleaner* claimed "Autoists Delighted With Parking Grounds." The article went on further to state that "[t]he many pretty compliments passed upon the auto parking grounds ought to be highly gratifying to the city fathers."

In her book *A Long Way from Boston*, Beth O'Shea recalled her visit to one of these camps:

> *"Is this a tourist camp?" I asked, looking around with interest. We had heard about them, but had expected something more elaborate.*
>
> *"Sure, it's a tourist camp," he told us. "Anythin's a tourist camp what has water and no no-trespass signs. All the towns has got 'em now. They figure they give you a place where you can pitch your tent and you'll buy food and stuff at their stores."*

But what sort of people stayed in these tourist camps? Norman S. Hayner, an associate professor of sociology at University of Washington, wrote in *Hotel Life*:

> *At home, each member of the organized or integrated family plays a role in the family interaction and this role is defined by the attitudes of the other members. When the family is touring, characteristic changes tend to occur in these roles and in the relationships between the different members. When the man takes a vacation from work, his wife frequently feels that she should have a vacation too, and as a result even in tourist camps the trend seems to be away from cooking and toward more "hotel service," i.e., having the beds made up in advance and the linen furnished. In the words of one auto camp owner an increasing number of his guests "don't carry a thing—only cigarettes" and those parties that do cook commonly buy a little stuff for supper—coffee for breakfast and away they go.*

Soon, amenities were added to the auto camps and tourist camps, small cottages and cabins were built and life on the road was geared toward

The owners of this 1920 Chevrolet Series 490 are taking a break at the covered picnic tables and fireplace. A collection of travel brochures and local maps is in the display on the post. The oak tree to the right still exists.

the car. The motel was born from combining the words "motor" and "hotel," and a billion-dollar industry was created to cater to the traveler.

The entrance to the camp was on the east side of Michigan Avenue under a small hastily built arbor and sign. It is clear that there is nothing in any of the images in this chapter that survives today except for the general direction and placement of the Dalton Wash (which now runs directly underneath the alley parking lot between the two buildings) and perhaps the big live oak tree to the south of the current parking lot. To the left of the entrance was a stone drinking fountain, an attractive addition to both passersby and camp visitors alike.

The camp patrons were provided sheltered picnic tables and several grand oak trees but very few amenities. The car in the image is a 1920 Chevrolet Series 490, which looks lightly loaded for any of the serious cross-country travel discussed previously. In addition, the license plate on the Chevrolet, "179-217," was a California plate only issued in 1921. If the picture were in color, the plate would have been yellow with black text, as the color scheme was changed each year.

In several of the pictures located in the Glendora Museum archives, there is an older man and woman seated at the picnic tables, and above

Three cars are parked in Glendora's Auto Camp in 1921, laden down with typical camping gear and equipment needed for a vacation. In the background is the Glendora Grace Episcopal Church on Vista Bonita, but at the time of this photograph, it was still a mission and not a full parish.

their heads is a sign that reads "Notice: For Your Convenience, Please Respect Accordingly." In the tiered box hanging on the post to the right of the couple is perhaps a collection of travel maps, Auto Club advertisements or brochures to local attractions. The top and bottom tiers clearly say "Glendora," but what is in them is uncertain—perhaps some information about the city or a brochure to the town's grocery stores and so on. Also notice that there is a small slot at the bottom of the display rack, and above the slot is a padlock. Since the camp was free, it is safe to assume that whatever brochures or maps they offered weren't free and that they collected for them on the honor system.

The dark wooden building with the cross on top in the background of the images is Glendora's Grace Episcopal Church on Vista Bonita. It was established in November 1910 with only five families—Brunjes, Vickery, Banholt, Delancy and Ward—and was the church Reverend Henry Scott Rubel presided over starting in October 1935. But when this picture was taken, in 1921, the church had yet to receive full parish status from the Diocese of Los Angeles, meaning that it was still considered a mission.

In a written account of the church in the 1960s by early parishioner Heidi Allen, she shared some memories:

> *In the little church on Vista Bonita—the bathroom was right on the other side of the wall from the credence table and on the same wall with the kitchen plumbing. Every time the toilet was flushed it could be heard throughout the church, and when the water in the kitchen was turned on (and there always seemed to be air in the pipes), that banging sound could also be heard. This was such a consternation that when the time came that we could plan our new church, everyone suggested that the altar and the plumbing be separated—which is probably the very reason why there is no plumbing in the Church proper. It was not an oversight, just over-compensating, I think.*

In 1954, the original church was moved to Mountain View Avenue, and in 1964 a new complex was consecrated.

According to a few sources—Donald Pflueger's book *Glendora* being one of them—the camp was closed in 1926 after a series of unrelenting problems, in addition to the proliferation of commercialized campgrounds. Constant commotion, vagrancy, noise and a general unkempt appearance of the camp were the main points cited, and it was probably argued that the land could better suit the needs of the community if it were used differently. It appears as though the temporary nature of the auto camp had degenerated into somewhat of a permanent situation for migrant workers during the picking seasons. Originally, the camps were meant for people who were traveling to the area for the first time and didn't have enough money to stay at a hotel; they could pitch a tent and spend a few nights before heading on with their trek. In a nutshell, the free place to stay was taken for granted.

But where has Route 66 gone? Tom Snyder summed up the loss of Route 66 in his book *Route 66: Traveler's Guide and Roadside Companion*: "No longer necessary to efficient cross-country travel, the road has been replaced by nine seamless interstate highways with no stoplights, no places of special interest, no appealing monstrosities. Just mile-by-mile progress in one direction or another. After the first few hours the ordinariness of it all is like watching a test pattern on television…Route 66 was never ordinary."

U.S. 66 was officially decommissioned (which means that it was officially removed from the United States Highway System) on June 27, 1985, after it was decided that the route was no longer relevant and had been replaced by the Interstate Highway System. Portions of the road that passed through Illinois, New Mexico and Arizona have been designated National Scenic Byways with the name "Historic Route 66."

In Glendora, one would be hard-pressed to find the name Alosta on any street signs in town anymore, as it was decided (to bolster interest and economic redevelopment to the Alosta corridor) that it would be renamed "Route 66." In a special meeting of the city council on July 9, 2002, Stan Wong, then director of planning and redevelopment for the city, introduced Ron Pflugrath, a planning manager at Robert Bein, William Frost & Associates (RBF) in Irvine, who was in charge of an eight-month "Route 66 Specific Plan," a project to convert the old Alosta corridor into what they now call the "Route 66 Business Corridor."

I'm sure that Bobby Troup would be pleased that, at least in Glendora, the Mother Road lives on forever.

The Santa Fe Comes to Glendora

W hat George Dexter Whitcomb and William Barstow Strong had in common were railroads, as they both had built their lives on the tracks, ties and locomotives, the future of transportation in a post–Civil War America. Strong, working his way up from the trenches of the business, eventually became the president of one of the largest railroad companies in the world, the Atchison, Topeka and Santa Fe Railway, in 1881. Under his control, Strong increased the line by more than seven thousand miles to not just be *one* of the largest railroad companies in the world, but *the* largest. Whitcomb took a slightly different route. He was more focused on the equipment, starting as a ticket taker for the Panhandle Railroad Company and then becoming a purchasing agent. This formed the groundwork in founding his own company, building locomotives and coal mining equipment.

The lives of the two men were quite parallel and even crossed paths several times. They both honed their skills in the railroad industry in which they made their fortunes, and they both controlled vast businesses and endured under great responsibility that took them from one side of the country to the other. They were both from Chicago, which was probably the most important detail to the history and success of Glendora.

By 1941, when this picture was taken, the Glendora Station along the AT&SF tracks had been in operation for nearly seventy-five years.

By 1885, Whitcomb and his family had arrived in what would soon be known as Glendora, and Strong's crews were skirting the deserts of California with his iron horses, carving a path toward Los Angeles via San Bernardino and the Cajon Pass, a formidable obstacle for both engineers and locomotives (even today).

The Southern Pacific, still a few years away from the big Central Pacific merger, had made its way down from San Francisco through Santa Clarita and Burbank, making for stiff competition over control of the freight and passengers pouring in and out of Southern California. According to *The Railroad Builders* by John Moody (1919), "To assure a connection with the coast in Southern California, the Santa Fe built a line to Colton, acquired the California Southern Railway from Colton to San Diego, and effected an entrance to Los Angeles by leasing the Southern Pacific tracks from Colton."

There was no question that railroads created civilization in their wakes, as new towns had sprung up along the tracks since they began laying down the rails in Kansas and Chicago. From *Urbanism and Empire in the Far West, 1840–1890*, Eugene P. Moehring wrote, "Train lines promoted urban development throughout the West, and southern California was no exception. The railroads either sired or nourished a new line of transshipment towns in the plains east of Los Angeles." Towns in the San Gabriel Valley "owed [their] success to farm products but more precisely to the Santa Fe Railroad, which carried these harvests to market." Moehring failed to mention that trains also brought people to these new towns, and Glendora wasn't disappointed.

The Atchison, Topeka and Santa Fe Railway wasn't the only game in town; rather, the railway system in Southern California was composed of a small collection of affiliate railroad companies that were either owned or had their tracks leased by the Santa Fe. California Southern Railroad was a subsidiary railroad that ran from National City (near San Diego) north to Barstow, while the San Bernardino and Los Angeles Railway was incorporated by the Santa Fe on November 20, 1886, to build a rail connection between San Bernardino and Los Angeles—a rail system right through what would be known as Glendora. Hanging on the wall of the Glendora Museum is an original map of George D. Whitcomb's dream for Glendora, showing a space for the new depot along the lines of the Santa Fe tracks. In that space, he wrote, "Depot Grounds of the LA&SB Branch of the AT&SF RR." It is interesting to note that he listed the railway incorrectly, as its official name is the San Bernardino and Los Angeles Railway (railroads are always named from east to west).

California Southern track crews performed the construction work, and the first train on the new line arrived in Los Angeles on May 31, 1887, so it is entirely accurate to say that the tracks that ran through Glendora were owned first by the San Bernardino and Los Angeles Railway and the California Southern Railroad, both subsidiaries of the Atchison, Topeka and Santa Fe Railway. More than likely, Whitcomb dealt more directly with the officials and engineers of the California Southern (Fred Perris, the chief engineer, specifically) than it did with those of the Santa Fe, but it is safe to say that the men of the California Southern didn't make a move without say so from AT&SF and that of William Barstow Strong.

A word on Fred Perris from the book *Fred Perris in Deseret* by Neil Jensen of the Perris Valley Historical and Museum Association:

> *Frederick Thomas Perris was born in Gloucester, England, January 21, 1837. He helped survey the Rancho San Bernardino and its sub-divisions. In the employ of the California Southern Railway Company, he practically built all of the lines comprising the Los Angeles division.*
>
> *During the latter part of 1882 he became Chief Engineer and Superintendent of Construction of the California Southern Railway (now the Los Angeles division of the AT&SF Railway). On September 13, 1883, he drove the first passenger train into San Bernardino and sounded the first locomotive whistle to be heard therein. In 1900 he was made manager of the Santa Fe's properties. He retired from service on a pension October 1, 1914, and died in 1916. While he never lived in Perris, the town, Perris Hill, and Perris Avenue were all named after Mr. Perris.*

Early in 1887, then, Whitcomb was more than likely south of his town site, working with Perris in securing the suggested route for the California

Starting out of an old boxcar on a rail siding in 1887, the Glendora Station was built later that year or in early 1888. The open platform on the right was later enclosed, and the whole structure was razed in the 1950s.

Southern tracks north of the South Hills. But it was Strong's word that drove the first spike on Whitcomb's land (and likely that of Gard's Alosta).

Just how the railroad ended up directly servicing Glendora is an interesting twist of history. The fact that AT&SF ran a line from San Bernardino to Los Angeles through Glendora would have been a moot point if it weren't for one man, J.F. Crank, the president the Los Angeles and San Gabriel Valley Railroad, a little thirty-one-mile length of track that reached Duarte. During the whole process of building his railroad, he was met with friction and outright refusal to help from the Southern Pacific (owned in part by the Big Four), as any railroad company within its "territory" was SP's rival and competitor.

In late 1886, Crank's shortline suddenly became hot property. Strong and the AT&SF were leasing SP tracks to reach Los Angeles, and the rates/terms weren't attractive enough to forestall his entering Los Angeles on AT&SF tracks instead of those of Huntington's Southern Pacific lines. In January 1887, Crank was invited both to Boston by the directors of the AT&SF and to Washington, D.C., by those of the SP to discuss the future of his line and a possible fortune for his coffers if he were to sell out to either one. Crank was in a unique position, being courted by two very wealthy pockets, but he had a specific agenda that would play out in his favor and that of Strong's.

If one were to look at a map of the Glendora area today, it is peculiar to note the route of the Santa Fe tracks as they snake across the San Gabriel Valley from San Bernardino. Roughly around the intersection of White and Arrow in LaVerne, the tracks make a slight northward jog toward San Dimas. This is a reasonable detour because of the need to circumvent the San Jose hills (where Puddingstone Lake is now), but instead of continuing along a westerly route through the south side of San Dimas and into Covina, following Arrow Highway toward Pasadena and eventually into Los Angeles, the tracks abruptly turn north. The tracks cross Gladstone, then Lone Hill and then what would be the 210 freeway, circling around the northeast corner of the South Hills before they straighten out and beeline into the heart of downtown Glendora. The biggest question is, then, why does it make such an awkward change in direction?

In November 1886, local residents could see surveying parties running lines west from the San Gabriel River toward Glendora. By the first week of January 1887, construction forces of the Los Angeles and San Gabriel Valley Railroad had crossed the San Gabriel River. At the same time, a gang of men was working westward from San Bernardino for the California Southern, and during the early part of 1887, the only topic of conversation was the coming railroad. A gap of only thirty-five miles remained, but what would be the route across the valley?

In February 1887, a dozen officials of AT&SF met with about twenty interested landowners (Whitcomb among them) in Frank P. Firey's office in Pomona to come to an agreement over the right-of-way of the tracks, as well as a decision on where stations were to be located. At this meeting, it was decided that the railroad would go through and stop at Glendora.

The engineers of the Santa Fe, specifically Fred Perris, could have saved themselves a lot of trouble if the tracks had just continued straight through San Dimas to the south of the South Hills, into Covina and on to Pasadena. But they didn't. There are several facts that remain.

Whitcomb knew Strong, but more importantly, Whitcomb was good friends with Charles W. Smith, the general manager and vice-president of the AT&SF, the man who likely called the shots on the day-to-day activities on the line. They had worked together in the offices of the Panhandle Railway in 1867, and it is likely that Smith was one of the representatives in Firey's Pomona office in February 1887.

There were several benefits to locating the tracks to the north of the South Hills. The ground was better, and there was a more reliable water source (for the engines) north of the South Hills. Before his work in railroads, Perris had been a city engineer (he laid out the grid of San Bernardino); Glendora and Azusa were plotted and more developed than the land south of the South Hills, thus making the land around the railroad (of which AT&SF owned a large portion) more desirable and hence more valuable. But probably the most determining factor was that it was a more direct line into the terminus of Crank's Los Angeles and San Gabriel Valley Railroad, the line's destination. After all, it would make sense to cross the San Gabriel River at its narrowest point, as this would require the shortest bridge and the most cost-efficient route. That would be as north as possible, a direct line from Azusa to Duarte. Before his work in railroads, Perris had acted as assistant engineer for James D. Schuyler of the State Engineering Department in measuring water in the valley of San Bernardino and locating the reservoir sites of both Big and Little Bear Valleys. He was a natural when it came to judging the lay of the land.

On May 31, 1887, the first Santa Fe train to travel over tracks owned and operated by Santa Fe arrived in Los Angeles, no doubt dropping off some visitors at the Glendora Station, then nothing but a converted boxcar.

The end result is that Glendora prospered, not just because of the wishes of Whitcomb or the desires of the newly arrived townspeople, but in large part because of the railroad. There were countless factors in play during the late 1880s that led to Glendora's success, and most is due to the moral foundation of the town, but to deny the railroad its due share of the success would be a mistake.

But what of the Santa Fe? In the February 1893 issue of *The Cosmopolitan* magazine (different from the one of the same name today), Charles S. Gleed wrote of the AT&SF railroad: "But the day came when the

There are only a few images of the second incarnation of the Glendora Station that survive. This cinder block building was constructed in the 1950s but didn't last too long. As of this writing, the land is empty and awaiting a new station for the expanding MetroLink.

traffic of the company was everywhere slaughtered by competition. In 1885, 1886 and 1887 the Missouri Pacific alone built 1,071 miles of road in the Santa Fe's immediate territory. In the same years the Chicago, Rock Island and Pacific road constructed about 1,300 miles also in the immediate territory of the Santa Fe."

Gleed later went on to sum up the whole experience of the railroad and the towns the sprang from it:

> *The romance involved in the history of the Santa Fe system can scarcely be more than hinted at here. There can never be again in this country such a life as was led by President Strong. Strictly within the bounds of civil life, he was yet as free as Columbus to discover new commercial worlds, declare war and wage it, organize and build communities, overturn political powers of long standing, replace old civilizations with new—and do all this asking no men's leave, save those whose money was to be risked, or those, few in number, whose tasks were somewhat like his and in the same field. Under his administration of the affairs of the Santa Fe Kansas was mostly settled, Colorado was developed, New Mexico was transformed, Arizona was awakened, Texas, California and Mexico were bound together, by way of Kansas, and all were guyed to the great western metropolis, Chicago. Towns were located and built, cities were brought into being, mines were opened, millions of people were moved, wars were waged and customs and precedents established in commerce and law. All this was done with one man as the chief arbitrator of many destinies.*

The Atchison, Topeka and Santa Fe Railway officially ceased operations on December 31, 1996, when it was merged with the Burlington Northern Railroad to form the Burlington Northern and Santa Fe Railway.

The once stately Victorian Glendora Station was torn down to make way for a block structure in the late 1950s. Very few pictures were taken of the second building before it, too, succumbed to the wrecking ball, and now the land lies in waiting for the third incarnation of train stations, that of the slowly expanding Gold Line of the MetroLink, due to reach Glendora by the mid-2010s.

The Weaver Building

The low-slung brick building on the southwest corner of Glendora and Meda Avenues fits in sedately with the block façades of most of the other storefronts in the downtown area, and it always has been overshadowed by the two relatively ornate buildings just to its south, the Gem and the First National Bank Building. In fact, most people don't look twice at it as they walk by, but it is well over one hundred years old and is one of the oldest structures still standing on Glendora Avenue.

Sadly, not much is known of its origins, aside that it is called the Weaver Building after its first owner and builder, Charles A. Weaver, a man responsible for building, financing or somehow supporting most every large-scale building on Michigan Avenue from 1905 to 1910: the opera house, the Gem Building, the Converse Building and, of course, the Weaver Building.

Soon after Weaver finished construction in about 1905 (or so it is suggested), he took an office in the back of the building for his real estate and insurance business: C.A. Weaver & Son. He also offered "money to loan" at "low rates."

However, the 1905 construction date of the Weaver Building is up for conjecture. In *The Making of the Glendora Library* by Kay Darlington (1999), she wrote that the Athena Club—which, along with the

On the corner of Meda and Glendora avenues sits the Weaver Building. Built in 1903, it housed a grocery store, hardware store and various restaurants over the last century. Here sits a 1907 Ford Model N, with (left to right) Charles Matthews, Clyde Wamsley and Charles Weaver in the background.

Glendora Woman's Club, was responsible for starting the Glendora Public Library—had a bake sale to raise money for a reading room in front of the Weaver Building sometime between December 1903 (when a reception was held to promote the project) and January 26, 1904 (when the reading room first opened). Darlington went on to list all of the possible locations for that reading room, including the use of the back rooms of the Weaver Building, as well as suggesting that Weaver himself gave the club a building in which to house the library, which seems mostly improbable. However, if Darlington's research is correct, the Weaver Building was there in 1903 at least.

There are two pictures of the Weaver Building included here in this chapter, and the photograph on the next page suggests an older building than previously thought. No extensively paved sidewalks. No light fixtures. No automobiles—just wagons, horses and hitching posts. It still has Wamsley in the picture (at left) and a caught-off-guard Matthews rubbing his eyes at just the wrong time.

Charles M. Matthews and Clyde Wamsley had been in business together since 1903 and were on the verge of ending their partnership. Wamsley wanted out of the grocery business, and after Matthews bought his share, Wamsley moved to Exeter to be near one of his brothers, Ed. In 1924, Matthews built a new store on the corner of Foothill and Vermont, Matthew's Grocery, and continued offering staples until 1936.

In a July 10, 1936 article titled "C.M. Matthews is Pioneer Merchant" in the *Glendora Gleaner*, the writer claimed that Matthews began his business with Wamsley in 1903. "Mr. Matthews was a member of the first of Matthews and Wamsley that opened the grocery store in a building where Reed's Hardware store is now located." It was also mentioned that by the time of that article, "[n]o other indivilual [*sic*] has been a merchant here as long as has Matthews."

Matthews & Wamsley's grocery store was in business in the corner of the Weaver Building for about seven years, until Wamsley sold out to Matthews, who moved his store to Foothill and Vermont in 1924.

On the other hand, the Wamsley family arrived in Glendora in 1891 and built a house on ten acres where Live Oak and Whitcomb meet (where Cullen School now stands). The patriarch of the family, James, was a Civil War veteran and still suffered from his wounds. In Glendora, he worked on the board of the first packinghouse, served on the school board and was the city's third postmaster, a job he kept for fifteen years. He married Bessie Cook and had four sons before making his way to California: Victor, Ed, Clyde and Frank. Ed built a house on the corner of Vista Bonita and Meda Avenues, later moving to a ranch in Exeter.

According to *Who's Who in the Pacific Southwest* (1913), Victor (his first name was Tyrone but he went by his middle name) graduated from Throop Polytechnic (later called Cal Tech) and became an architect in Glendora until about 1911, when he organized the Valley Vehicle and Tool Company. His offices were located in the Wood Building. Fourth brother, Frank, also studied at Throop but later went to the Beaux Arts Institute in Chicago and studied art under Solon Borglum (younger brother of Gutzon, of Mount Rushmore fame). Frank was an aerial photographer during World War I, and according to *Artists in California, 1786–1940*, his specialties were fountains, garden and architectural sculptures. None is known to still exist. Of course, Clyde became a grocer.

The main photograph in this chapter (page 126) is interesting on several different levels. Matthews is standing on the left, and Wamsley, in the wide-brimmed hat, is looking forlorn and very much like his father, James. He stares down the camera in the center (in both pictures actually), and Charles Weaver is standing on the right.

The most prominent feature in the picture is the car in the foreground, a rather well-used 1907 Ford Model N. By afternoon—this picture was probably taken at about 2:00 p.m., judging by the shadows—the photographer decided that it was too hot for a heavy coat, so he slung it over the back of his car seat and snapped the shutter.

There are a few signs hanging on the building. One notes that "Home telephone service will return on Monday," while another is a want ad for a public stenographer, posted by R.L. Bidwell, Glendora's first attorney. Bidwell arrived in Glendora from the Temescal Canyon area (Corona and Temecula) on September 1, 1903, and quickly made a name for himself as a community leader and influential businessman, as well as one of the largest benefactors in the history of the Glendora Public Library. Apparently, when this picture was taken, Bidwell was in need of a stenographer, and Glendora had phone service (about 130 phones, as it were).

A closer look at the photograph provides a wealth of clues to when it was taken. The Home Telephone Company began to provide phone service to Glendorans in 1902; Bidwell arrived in town and the building was suspected of being built in 1903; and 1907 was when the Ford Model N was brand new (which it clearly isn't).

But there are three more clues, one obvious and the other two quite subtle, and the funny thing about these particular clues is that they contradict one another, especially in relation to the other items in the picture. The obvious clue is the American flag hanging in the window. It is a forty-five-star flag, shown by its alternating rows of seven and eight stars, a flag that was officially used from July 4, 1896 (with the addition of Utah) to July 4, 1908, after Oklahoma joined the Union in November 1907. It would stand to reason that this picture was taken sometime before July 4, 1908, as it is certain that men of the caliber of Wamsley and Matthews would be acquainted with current events of that magnitude.

However, it appears as though they weren't, especially since there is a calendar hanging on the wall in the office on the right, and it is quite clear that the fourth day of this month is a Saturday. So, Saturday the fourth, in what year and what month? In the window on the left, where "Groceries" is painted, is a small sign that notes "Just a Few After Christmas Bargains." That could only mean that it is sometime after Christmas in a month that the fourth day falls on a Saturday, and there are only two possibilities that would make sense out of this sign: January 1908 or December 1909.

However, there is one more thing. Look above Mr. Wamsley (the man in the middle) in the leaves of the pepper tree. There's an electric light hanging on the side of the building, a feature that was only possible after April 9, 1908, because an article on April 16 in the *Glendora Gleaner* noted: "How did you like the electrical lights on the Opera House Thursday, April 9? Did it occur to your mind to record

By about 1917, Charles Weaver had moved his business from the back of his building to the front (seen in this picture of Michigan Avenue) and added his son to the title. By this time, he was also selling automobiles as a local agent of the Empire Automobile Company.

the date when electricity was first used for lighting purposes in your own beautiful city of Glendora?"

So, the photograph at the beginning of this chapter was taken in December 1909, but what doesn't make sense is the flag. It is clearly outdated, given the facts and clues found in other parts of the picture. Perhaps they didn't see a need to buy a new one just yet; after all, New Mexico and Arizona would be added in three short years.

It isn't clear when Matthews left the Weaver Building, and perhaps he merely downsized after Wamsley retired, but by about 1917, Weaver had moved to the corner office at the front of the building.

At about this time, Weaver added automobile sales to his repertoire of land and loans. In a 1917 advertisement, he hawks his new wares: "The 3 Styles of Automobiles manufactured by the Empire Automobile Co. are: 6-cylinder Cruiser $1275; 4-cylinder Yacht, $1100; 6-cylinder Launch, $1295. Latest models ready for your inspection. C.A. Weaver, Local Agent."

By 1927, James Reed had been in Glendora operating a hardware store for four years. When the three buildings on the corner of Meda and Michigan Avenues (essentially the Weaver Building) went up for sale, he bought them and converted them into two stores, one for his hardware store and the other as a rental. A few years later, he remodeled both stores in order to have a sporting goods store in addition to his hardware store. He was joined by his son, Roland, and together they formed a father-son business partnership for many years. It wasn't without some excitement, of course. In a September 27, 1954 *Time* magazine article on crime, the writer reported on a holdup at Reed's Hardware, no doubt in the sporting goods side: "In Glendora, Calif., a man walked into Reed's Hardware Store, asked to see a .45-cal. automatic, was shown a $65 model, admiringly loaded it, pointed it at the clerk, walked out with $41 and the pistol."

Now the Weaver Building, aka Reed's Hardware, is Frisella's Roastery. The building, itself a slight fraction of its former glory of 1903, has been stripped of its decorative stonework, cornices and artistic embellishments.

The Big Tree

O ne of Glendora's little-known landmarks is older than most everything in the city and nearly as old as Glendora itself. Tucked away on a small parcel of land at the corner of Santa Fe and Colorado Avenues, the Big Tree Park features the largest tree in Glendora and perhaps one of the largest trees in Southern California.

What is affectionately and aptly named the Big Tree is, in fact, a Moreton Bay Fig (its botanical name is *Ficus macrophylla*), originally a native plant of Australia. Interestingly enough, it is a strange tree with a bipolar disorder, as it is well adapted at being able to take on two forms, a full-fledged tree or a vine. If the germinating seed is allowed to fall onto the ground, it takes root and grows up into a magnificent tree reaching an enormous size. However, it is more likely that a fig seed will get eaten by a bird and deposited in the trunk or boughs of another tree, where something altogether different happens.

According to John Dunmore Lang in his 1852 book *An Historical and Statistical Account of New South Wales*: "This tree bears a species of fig, which I was told (for it was not in season at the time) is by no means unpalatable, and of which it seems the natives and the bronze-winged pigeons of the Australian forest are equally fond. As soon…as these tendrils reach the earth, they all successively strike root into the soil. Nothing in the

The Moreton Bay Fig was planted by Edgar J. Owens in 1890 on land perhaps leased from John P. Hanes.

Australian forest can long resist the fatal embrace of the native fig-tree, and the tree around which it has thus sprung into parasitical life is doomed eventually to die."

The exact story behind this particular Moreton Bay Fig and how it ended up towering above this plot of land in Glendora is somewhat of a mystery. It has been recorded in the *Glendora Press-Gleaner* from the 1950s that it was planted by Edgar J. Owens in 1890, but it doesn't state whether he was the one who imported it from Australia. From land records, the portion of land on which the tree now resides was owned by John P. Hanes in 1884. Perhaps Owens, of whom little is known, leased the land.

Regardless, the land soon became the front yard of Arthur Bohnard, a local watercolor artist whose talents and paintings have faded out of existence. A note on the back of a popular postcard of the tree states that it was planted in front of the Whisler House, a gingerbread-style house that sat too close to the ever-broadening tree. It was removed and the last of Glendora's orange groves destroyed for urban development (which led the way for the organization of the Glendora Preservation Foundation in the 1980s). As it stands now, the Big Tree takes up about one-third of its allotted 7,500-square-foot park.

The Moreton Bay Fig, according to Ferdinand von Mueller's book *Extra-Tropical Plants Readily Eligible for Industrial Culture or Naturalization*, written in 1884, is "perhaps the grandest of Australian avenue trees, and among the very best to be planted, although in poor dry soil its growth is slow. In the latitude of Melbourne it is quite hardy in the lowland. The foliage may occasionally be injured by grasshoppers. Easily raised from seed."

In N. Maisondau's 1912 book *Down Under*, he shared one of the fates of the massive trees: "Specimens of these trees are all to be seen in and about Sydney, but the most beautiful shade trees of its streets, and the finest of its Park trees, are the Moreton Bay Figs. These curious,

Ernest Benjamin Gray took this photograph of the Big Tree in 1910 in the front yard of local watercolor artist Arthur Bohnard. That same year, Gray earned recognition as a master photographer after his photographs were showcased on the cover of twelve consecutive issues of a Los Angeles magazine. He came to be known as the official photographer of the Mount Wilson resorts, and his postcards helped to popularize the mountain resorts of Southern California.

massive trunks, surmounted by dense, beautiful foliage, meet one at every turn, and so frequently outgrow their allotted space, that they must be sacrificed...There is no room for them now in the growing cities."

The Big Tree had been enjoying a solitary life in a vacant lot at 655 South Santa Fe Avenue for a few decades until it was purchased by Dr. Edward McNamara. Soon thereafter, in September 1971, the property was acquired by the American Medical Enterprise Inc. (AME), the parent company that owns the then named Glendora Community Hospital, with plans of expanding the hospital at the ultimate sacrifice of the tree.

The tree was saved, not because an outcry erupted from the city (very few knew of the hospital's plans) but because AME hadn't completely decided what to do with the property and, in the interim, suggested instead that it would make a decent park. At this time, Ron Hanson, then a young employee of the Parks and Recreation Department, helped broker a deal that would eventually save the tree for future generations. In the introduction memo to a report prepared by Hanson in 1971 about the prospect of a new park at the location, he suggested a few alternatives: "The reason for AME's purchase was for purposes of future expansion of their hospital facilities which presently occupy the square block immediately east of the tree. Because this expansion will be at an undetermined future date, they have expressed a desire to develop the lot into a small park."

Hanson listed nine benefits of converting the property into a park, from "creating a relaxing and intimate atmosphere for hospital patients" to "promoting greater awareness of the tree by the public." Also mentioned was the greatest obstacle in front of the Big Tree's ability to survive the 1970s: "Ownership of the land is vested with AME, a profit motivated corporation, not primarily interested in developing recreational areas for the general public." An honest assessment of most companies, but AME did something unusual. Later in the year, the city was given an easement on the tree and its surrounding land, as long as it always remains a park and as long as Glendora foots the bill for its maintenance and development.

Hanson estimated that the cost of the project would be about $7,500, with the largest percentage of that going to tree surgery, as some cables were installed to support a few of the lower branches. This work was done by Western Arborists of Pasadena. The director then of the Parks and Recreation Department, George Manooshian (a park bearing his name now exists at the southwest corner of Loraine and Palm Avenues), said of the Big Tree: "The tree is a very healthy one. We haven't needed to spray it or give it any special care."

The project took six years and more than $10,000 to complete. The tree was dedicated and officially hailed as Big Tree Park on April 26, 1975, and one year later, as part of Glendora's bicentennial festivities, the neighboring lot was purchased and on it were planted six redwood trees donated by the James Muir family. Because of vandalism, only three have survived.

In his book *Ficus: The Exotic Species*, Dr. Ira J. Condit wrote: "A tree…at Glendora, California, with a girth of 8.25 meters above the buttresses, is regarded as the largest of its kind in California." It is surprising to think

Glendora residents Pat Zaffiras and Connie Adams are shown here enjoying the shade of the Big Tree in this 1952 image.

that Condit hadn't heard of another Moreton Bay Fig, one located in Santa Barbara, once on the property of the famous Potter Hotel. That particular fig, measuring about 120 feet across, is considered the largest of its kind in California, which puts Glendora's tree a close second.

In *Material Dreams: Southern California through the 1920s* by Kevin Starr (1990), he wrote: "Everything about the Potter was larger than life, including the gigantic Morton Bay Fig Tree on one edge of the property. Planted in 1877, the tree had grown to a trunk circumference of 31 feet by the early 1900s. Its branches extended over half the size of a modern football field. As the largest fig tree in the world, the Moreton Bay Fig Tree stood as a perfect complement to the Potter, one of the largest hotels in the country."

Another Moreton Bay Fig, this one closer to home, resides at 11000 National Boulevard in Los Angeles. It was planted two years before the Potter tree, supposedly by the Smith family to shade their La Balloona Ranch cottage. It is now part of the property owned by the St John's Presbyterian Church in Westdale.

A few words about the photographer of the postcard used in this chapter: Ernest Benjamin Gray was born in Cuyahoga Falls, Ohio, in 1874. As a young man he came to California and became interested in outdoor photography. In about 1910, he gained recognition as a photographer after his work was showcased on the cover of twelve consecutive issues of a Los Angeles magazine, and he eventually came to be known as the official photographer of the Mount Wilson resorts. He published many of his prints as postcards, and this helped to popularize the mountain resorts of Southern California.

Gray lived in Sierra Madre, spending much of his time in the San Gabriel Mountains. He and his wife, Marguerite, ran the Little Gray Inn on the Sturtevant Trail. In 1927, the inn burned down, destroying some of Gray's equipment and photographic plates.

In 1930, E.B. Gray and his family moved from Sierra Madre to Idyllwild, a mountain community in the San Bernardino National Forest. For ten years, Gray ran a photography and gift shop in the center of Idyllwild, and after his death in 1940, his son, Bob, took over the business.

The Converse Tragedies

The account of the Converse Building is as straightforward as any two-story building in the downtown area or any mildly interesting office building of the era. It has cinder blocks, concrete, paint, windows, storefronts and office spaces—nothing outstanding, no major milestones were passed architecturally speaking and the building itself only added to the character of Glendora's skyline. However, it is the unusual and lesser-known tragedy of the Converse family that presents itself as the real story behind the Converse Building. It involves a Mexican revolution, espionage, an international incident, three generations of accidental deaths, Senate subcommittee hearings and polygamy…all in Glendora.

The family name Converse comes from old French, meaning "convert," and was given to those of Jewish descent who converted to Christianity. In 1847, on their farm in Iowa, one of Erastus and Elizabeth Converse's sons became desperately ill, and Erastus rode seventy miles on a horse without a saddle to fetch a doctor. Either the ride was strenuous or he was too exposed to the elements, because upon his return Erastus died suddenly from his ordeal, beginning the tragedy that would befall three of the next four generations of Converse men.

After Erastus's death, William Converse (born on October 20, 1833) inherited the family ranch and remained there to take care of his mother

Built by successful lawyer Charles Henry Converse in 1905 to house his law offices (upstairs), the Converse Building has gone through many changes over the last one hundred years that have rendered it mostly unrecognizable compared to its original form. The WCTU drinking fountain was built in 1909.

and younger siblings. He was seventeen years old and was able to find work in the army as a driver and a cook while Fort Gaines was being built in Minnesota. At the age of nineteen in 1851, William married Jane C. Henry (age fifteen), a native of Ohio, and they raised a family of six children. He served in the army until 1871, when he sold the family homestead and moved to Valley Township in Pottawattamie County, Iowa.

William and Jane's third child, Charles Henry Converse, was born in Iowa in February 1856. When Charles was twenty-four, he met and married Alice S. Strong (also from Iowa), and they moved to California to live with his uncle, John, in Coulterville. There, Charles worked as a teacher and is listed in the September 27, 1879 edition of the *Mariposa Gazette* as one of the fourteen teachers who attended the Mariposa County Teachers Institute. They had their first son, Earnest Lloyd, in 1883.

Also of note during this time is the Converse family's involvement in the exploration and settling of the California Sierra Nevadas, as Uncle John and William helped finance and build a railroad near Yosemite. As a result, several places are named after the Converse family—Converse Ferry across the San Joaquin River and the heavily logged Converse

Basin, for example. Perhaps Alice grew tired of "frontier" life or an existence in the era after the gold rush or perhaps some unknown marital strife drove them apart, but they divorced sometime before 1889, when Charles Henry moved back to Iowa and married Flora Emma Manley from Illinois. There they had four more children (Lawrence, Hazel, Gertrude and Flora) before moving back to California, this time settling in Glendora just after 1900.

It is unclear when or where Charles became an attorney, but by the time he had returned to California and taken up residence in Glendora, he was operating a very successful law firm in Los Angeles County. He was successful enough to commission a modest two-story Italian-style building on Michigan Avenue to house his law offices upstairs and several businesses downstairs. The building, of course, is the Converse Building, built in 1905.

Two of his four children (Earnest Lloyd and Hazel) both followed in his footsteps, became lawyers and lived well into their nineties. The second son, Lawrence Floyd Converse, took a slightly different course in life. Not much is known about the short life of Lawrence, except that he was born in Avoca, Iowa, in December 1889 and attended one year of Harvard Military School in Los Angeles (established in 1900 by Grenville C. Emery). When just twenty-two years old, Lawrence found himself in Texas and Mexico, involved in the Mexican Revolution of 1910.

The revolution was brought about by social unrest under the dictatorship of President Porfirio Díaz, who had been in office for thirty-one years. Francisco I. Madero created the "Anti-Reelectionista" Party and campaigned heavily for the removal of Díaz and the installation of a truly democratic government. Shortly before the elections of 1910, Madero was apprehended in Monterrey and imprisoned in San Luis Potosi, with Díaz reelected soon after. Upon his release, Madero was exiled to the United States and issued the "Plan of San Luis," declaring the election a fraud and himself president pro tem. Madero's call for an uprising on November 20, 1910, marked the beginning of the Mexican Revolution.

During this time, Lawrence Converse and other Americans involved themselves in the revolution and were captured by Díaz's army in Juarez. On February 20, 1911, at the home of Melquisiades Perea on the north side of Rio Grande about five miles south of the Tomillo Station on the Santa Fe, Texas and Southern Railroad, Converse and Edwin M. Blatt were captured by Díaz's troop and taken south across the river. They were told that they had violated neutrality laws (which they undoubtedly had) and that they'd be shot in the morning.

The result of their capture and imprisonment boiled into an international incident, as Lawrence and Blatt defended their innocence and claimed that they were captured on American land. Because of testimony from many witnesses at the Perea house, personal items of Converse and Blatt that were found in their captors' possession and evidence of their fire on the Perea property, Díaz was forced to release the prisoners. It also helped that Lawrence's father, Charles Henry, had been an acquaintance with Díaz himself (through the help of Harrison Gray Otis, of the *Los Angeles Times*) and was able to expedite his son's release.

Soon after he was freed, Lawrence met and married Amelia Sara Spencer in El Paso, and she gave birth to Lawrence Jr. on April 17, 1912, in California. Less than one month later, on May 4, 1912, Charles Henry Converse was crossing the Santa Fe tracks at Loraine Avenue in Glendora when he was struck and killed by a fast-approaching train. According to the May 6, 1912 edition of the *New York Times*, "There is a considerable grade where the Santa Fe tracks cross Loraine Avenue and it is believed that Mr. Converse turned on oil to make the grade and drowned out his engine." The *Mariposa Gazette* on May 11 noted: "After being struck, his body was carried along the tracks for a quarter of a mile before the train was brought to a standstill." Charles Henry Converse was fifty-four years old and is buried at the Oakdale Cemetery in the family plot.

In September 1912, Lawrence Converse and the other Americans who were involved in the Mexican Revolution were called to El Paso to testify in the Senate hearings regarding the revolution and their involvement. Though Converse was accused of being a traitor, he wasn't charged with any crime and returned to Glendora and his late father's orchards. There in the large rock-adorned house on Sierra Madre, Converse's life began to change. Perhaps the death of his father was an emotional blow or perhaps the accusations brought against him by Congress wounded him, but Lawrence's actions after May 1912 delve into the strange and surreal.

He fled the country with his wife and baby, taking up residence in Havana, Cuba, where his second son, John Charles, was born in 1913. Soon thereafter, the family returned to Los Angeles. It is unknown whether he returned to Glendora, but there is evidence that his family still had ties here at that time. In a picture of the Converse Building taken after the time of Charles Henry's death, a sign on building notes "E.L. Converse, Lawyer," which was Charles's oldest son, Earnest Lloyd. Hazel Converse maintained her law practice in Arcadia but no doubt spent time in Glendora; this is where she was later buried. Incidentally, after Charles Henry's death, his wife, Flora, married a lawyer who swindled her out of the family's orchards in Glendora and then divorced her. She then married John Hussong, who started the famous cantina (where the margarita was invented) in Ensenada, Mexico. During prohibition, Flora and John ran liquor across the border in a secret compartment in the trunk of their car.

The part of Lawrence's life after he returned to Southern California remains shrouded in controversy and multiple (and conflicting) stories. Somehow, Lawrence met Barbara LaMarr, a young burlesque dancer who would become one of the first people to make it rich in Hollywood, as well as one of the first to die a drug-related death. Born in Yakima, Washington, in 1896, her parents moved her to Los Angeles, and she was a burlesque dancer by the age of fourteen. From there, it didn't take her long to get into trouble. She was arrested for dancing in a burlesque show, which provoked a juvenile court judge to remark that she was "too beautiful to be in a big city alone and unprotected." (Studio publicists later seized the phrase and trumpeted her as "the Girl Who Is Too Beautiful.") Three years later, in 1914, she ran away from home, returned to burlesque dancing and married Texas rancher Jack Lytell (who died a few months later).

That same year, on June 2, she married Lawrence Converse. No sooner had the ink dried on the marriage certificate (on which they signed false names) than Lawrence was hauled away in handcuffs and thrown in jail for bigamy. Of course, he was still married to Amelia and had two young children, a fact that he conveniently forgot, according to testimony at his trial/hearing.

According to an article written by 1920s Broadway star Elsie Ferguson:

> *Lawrence Converse testified in court that the first time he met her, he found her beauty so startling that it obliterated from his mind the fact that he was already married. He claimed emotional amnesia. He testified in court that Barbara's beauty caused a blood clot, creating pressure on his brain. To remove the clot, doctors in Los Angeles operated on him. Before he was hauled off to that fatal operating table, his final words were: "Tell Barbara that I will always love her through eternity."*

This particular version of his death is also referenced in the *Los Angeles Times*.

Another account notes that Converse, so despondent by being arrested and forlorn by the separation of his new wife, repeatedly banged his head on the bars and walls of his jail until he was rendered unconscious, all the while wailing for LaMarr. As a result, the blood clot was formed that subsequently caused his death.

One more report is sourced directly from living relatives of Lawrence; they said that in July 1914, a full month after the bigamy charges, he dove into a swimming pool, hit his head on the bottom and was killed quite instantly. Whichever story is true, he is buried with his parents and siblings in Oakdale, and as for Lawrence's widow, Amelia, she moved back to El Paso, Texas, to live with her mother until about 1920 and then married a man by the name of Ralph C. Payne, living out her life until her death in 1959. Interestingly, in 1923, nine years after the LaMarr affair and his death, Amelia tried to claim $25,000 in compensation from Mexico for the wrongful imprisonment of her husband. It was denied, stating that Converse had caused his own suffering by taking part in the revolution

Throughout it all, the Converse Building weathered the storms, the scandals and the gossip. Its longest early tenant was the Fountain Confectionery Shop (started probably after 1909, or at least renamed then), which sold ice cream, John J. Ingalls cigars, Rough House Chocolates, Armour's Malted Clams and delicious-sounding Armour Hot Beef Tea. Upstairs, to the south of the Converse law offices, were

Started sometime after 1909, the Fountain Confectionery Shop sold a wide variety of items, from ice cream to cigars and tea-flavored drinks.

the offices of the Glendora Water Company and the Glendora Irrigation Company, and on the corner ground floor space was J.W. McGraw and Sons, a grocery and dry goods store, as well as a men's clothing store.

In the front, erected by the Woman's Christian Temperance Union in 1909, was the drinking fountain (for horses on the street side and people on the sidewalk side). It only lasted until about 1920, when the decline of horsepower (replaced by less thirsty automobiles) caused it to be removed—it was also possibly a result of the newly paved Michigan Avenue.

Sometime after 1920, the law offices were gone, as well as the water and irrigation offices. Dr. Wood opened his offices where the water and irrigation companies had been. The Fountain Confectionery, despite lacking its namesake fountain, was moved to the middle space, making room for a watchmaker's shop on the south corner.

During World War II, the Fountain Confectionery space was vacated, as were most of the offices upstairs. A five-and-dime was opened where the watchmaker's shop was, but the rest sat shuttered for some time.

The building was completely refurbished by Helen and Eddie Nelson twenty years after they took ownership of it in 1943. More changes were to come in later years.

In 1943, Helen and Eddie Nelson moved their pharmacy business from the Finance Building on the corner of Michigan and Foothill Boulevard to 159 North Glendora Avenue, the Converse Building, calling it Nelson's Drug Store. In about 1965, the building was completely refurbished, stripped of its Italian façade, its cornices and its overhanging corner offices. After Eddie's death in 1976, Helen sold the pharmacy to the Lee family. The building was renamed the Lee Building, and the business has been in the family ever since.

Frank Chance in Glendora

Frank LeRoy Chance was born on September 9, 1877, to William Harvey Chance and Mary Russell. The Chance family came to California via covered wagon from Missouri in 1846. Out on his own in 1862, William farmed rented land near Stockton and, six years later, had moved to Stanislaus County to farm on his own land. Soon, William and Mary moved from Stanislaus County to Fresno to expand his farming to include ranching. By the time Frank was born, the Chance family was quite wealthy, living in a well-to-do home at 837 O Street in Fresno. A few years later, William was delving into real estate and proving to be a successful and smart investor. He was one of the largest stockholders in the First National Bank of Fresno, as well as its director and vice-president for a number of years, but his health began to decline. He died in 1892 at the age of fifty-two.

As a young boy, Frank discovered that he had a fondness for a new sport called baseball, and in 1888, eleven-year-old Frank was a member of the first organized "kid" team in Fresno. The desire to be a "real" team and not just play on dirt lots and empty fields motivated them to approach W.H. Daniels, the head of circulation at the *Fresno Evening Expositor*. The publisher of the paper encouraged sports among kids and okayed the sponsorship, and as a result of their organization, the team beat almost every other team encountered, from Visalia and Madera to Merced and Tulare. The newspaper was so impressed that it offered to hire any of the boys to the circulation department, and most of them jumped at the chance.

There exists in the archives of the Fresno paper a picture of the team in 1889, and since Frank Chance was the smallest boy on the team, the photographer had him lie down in front of the first row. Along with the photo, the November 27, 1889 issue reported on the team's latest game, noting that Frank played

Frank LeRoy Chance lived in Glendora for only a dozen years or so and used his property on Grand Avenue as an off-season home until his death in 1924.

first base and Frank Homan (who would later become his brother-in-law) played catcher. As far as Frank's studies, he was a good student, and he met his future wife, Edythe Pancake, in high school, where he spent many hours studying with her. Other than this, his early career is speckled.

The *New York Evening World* reported of his exploits on the baseball team as catcher for Washington College in Irvington, California, from 1893 to 1895. In subsequent articles from the *Evening World*, it has him playing semipro ball in Illinois for forty dollars per month, and then in 1897, the *Evening World* reported him back in college playing the catcher for the Fresno Republican Tigers, another semipro team. In a book called *Los Angeles from the Mountains to the Sea*, the writer confirmed that Frank attended Washington College for three years and then went to Illinois, finally returning to Fresno at the request of his mother. Once home, he went to work in a doctor's office but continued to play in local tournaments. Confusion continued when the November 3, 1906 issue of

Sporting Life had Frank going to Washington College and then obtaining a dental degree at the Dental College in San Francisco. Still others suggest that he went to Berkeley. But what is most important to the story is that he never gave up baseball.

In 1897, he was playing with the Fresno Republican Tigers and hit an impressive .479 in the Examiners State League tournament, a batting average that attracted talent scouts from the Major Leagues. It wasn't long before the Chicago National League signed him to a contract, and even though Baltimore had outbid Chicago by $300, Chance liked Chicago and knew that the team's current catcher, Tim Donohue, was out of action because of an injured thumb. His starting salary was $1,200 a year, an unheard-of figure, especially since Chance was one of the few people to get into the big leagues straight from the amateurs without any minor-league experience.

Frank Chance's big break in baseball came soon after he arrived at West Baden Springs, Indiana, to play for the Chicago Colts in 1898. The team's longtime manager, Cap Anson, left, and soon reports were referring to them as the Chicago Orphans, a nicknamed that stuck, and since the team lacked proper leadership, Chance was given some opportunities. His first game was on April 29, 1898, against Louisville, but Chance started out on the benches because Tim Donohue decided to play through the pain of his thumb. In the last inning, management pulled out Donohue and let Chance crouch behind home plate for exactly two outs. It was unremarkable to the fans and essentially had no effect on the game (the Orphans won 16–4), but it must have been exhilarating to Frank.

His career was born, but it wasn't without trouble. In 1900, Frank Chance ran into prizefighter Jim Corbett at Corbett's Broadway café, and though the circumstances are unclear, Chance accused Corbett of fixing the fight between him and Kid McCoy. His accusations caused a scuffle that broke out into a brawl, and when spring training got underway that season, his new nickname became "Husk," one that he didn't seem to mind at all.

Meanwhile, he proposed to Edythe Pancake, but they were hesitant about getting married. It was the start of a new season, and Frank was a little self-conscious that he would even have a job to return to, much less one in Chicago. Frank was now a second-string catcher after the mended

Donohue took the plate. Plus, when he did marry Edythe, he told her that he didn't want her living in a small apartment next to the ball field but rather in a grand house befitting his growing stature. They decided to wait, and while they did, he returned home to Fresno to give away his sister, Stella, to his old friend and ex-teammate, Frank Homan.

By 1905, the Orphans had long since come to be called the Cubs and were about to take their place among the premier teams in baseball history. Along with stationing Chance at first base, then manager Selee had brought up second baseman Johnny Evers and shortstop Joe Tinker, who were soon to join Chance in becoming the most celebrated infield trio in the game's history. It was this "Tinker to Evers to Chance" that made him a star, immortalized by Franklin Adams in the poem "Baseball's Sad Lexicon" first published in the *New York Evening Mail* on July 10, 1910:

> *These are the saddest of possible words:*
> *"Tinker to Evers to Chance."*
> *Trio of bear cubs, and fleeter than birds,*
> *Tinker and Evers and Chance.*
> *Ruthlessly pricking our gonfalon bubble,*
> *Making a Giant hit into a double—*
> *Words that are heavy with nothing but trouble:*
> *"Tinker to Evers to Chance."*

Chance's great success came as a young manager. He was twenty-seven when he took over the Chicago club from Frank Selee in mid-1905; in four out of seven full seasons, he won at least 100 games per season and never finished lower than third. His .664 winning percentage (768-389) stands as the best in Cubs history. In 1906, the Cubs won 116 games—a major-league record—while losing just 36. They lost to the White Sox in the 1906 World Series but defeated the Tigers in the next two. Chance led all participants in the 1908 World Series with a .421 batting average.

Chance moved on to the Yankees in 1913, but ill health forced him to retire with New York in seventh place in 1914. He returned to his native California and owned and managed the Los Angeles (Pacific Coast League) team in 1916–17. He returned east in 1923 to try to rebuild

This picture of the Chance Building was taken soon after it was built in 1912. J.J. Peyton's Cub Grocery and Jim Maloney's Cub Pharmacy were longtime occupants of the ground floor.

the Red Sox, decimated by the sale of stars (including Babe Ruth) to the Yankees, but they finished in last place.

In 1946, Chance, Joe Tinker and Johnny Evers, three men who really didn't like one another but were linked together by a remarkable play, were inducted into the Hall of Fame.

In 1910, Chance (along with Charles A. Comiskey) wrote a book called *The Bride and the Pennant: The Greatest Story in the History of America's National Game*, and also during this time, he took up residence in Glendora, building what was known as Cub Ranch on Grand Avenue, just north of Baseline. He owned an orange grove and no doubt used some of his money (as well as some of his father's) to build the Chance Building on the northeast corner of Michigan Avenue and Foothill Boulevard in 1912, after he was fired from the Cubs but before he started with the Yankees.

The Chance Building has gone through very little transformation in the one hundred years since its construction, but there has been a steady stream of shops and stores throughout the years. Most of the early ones, the Cub Pharmacy (operated by Jim Maloney) and Cub Grocery (owned

On December 17, 1990, a fire broke out in one of the upstairs apartments of the Chance Building. Although the fire consumed most of the second floor, it was reconstructed a year later.

by J.J. Peyton) for example, celebrated the origins of the building, but by the early 1930s, with the advent of Turner's Café and Soda Shop, which replaced the Cub Pharmacy, as well as Glendora Hardware taking up residence to the north, most connections to Frank Chance were lost.

In fact, the building just melted into the subtle skyline of Glendora, mostly forgotten, with a few small shops occupying the lower level and converted apartments along the second floor. It didn't come to public attention until December 17, 1990, when a fire broke out in one of the apartments, consuming most of the second floor. The building was decidedly unsafe and underwent a complete renovation for earthquake retrofitting and structural reinforcement.

As for Frank LeRoy Chance, his name is mostly lost to the history of Glendora, only being attached to a building that no longer bears his name as prominently as when it was first built. He briefly returned to baseball in 1924 to manage the White Sox, but his health worsened and he died that September.

Chance was forty-seven years old.

Glendora's 1937
Get-Together

The Glendora Golden Get-Together parade was held on Saturday May 29, 1937, and was part of a weekend-long program of events. Kicked off by Grand Marshal Leonard G. Shelton at the head of the parade on a palomino, the parade started at 2:00 p.m. on that particularly overcast and misty spring day.

The Friday, June 4, 1937 edition of the *Glendora Press-Gleaner* claimed that there were between 10,000 and 15,000 people lining the parade route (the *Los Angeles Times* declared more than 20,000, but then again, it called Michigan Avenue Main Street), which is an impressive turnout, considering that the 1940 census shows fewer than 2,800 people lived in all of Glendora at the time.

An interesting note to add is that the parade route was inexplicably changed at the last minute and failed to follow the "march" laid out by the planners. Original plans called for the parade to head south on Michigan from Leadora, turn west on Foothill to Vermont, then south to Carroll, east to Michigan again, north to Foothill and finally east to Wabash, where it would end up at the ballpark and the Pacific Electric tracks (which is now known as Finkbiner Park). Instead, the parade turned east on Foothill from Michigan and went directly to Wabash and the ballpark, hardly the two miles that was boasted in the paper.

Many felt cowboy hats were sold to spectators along the parade route. This example, part of the Glendora Historical Society's collection in the museum, was signed by many prominent citizens of the day.

In all, there were 114 entries and floats, "countless" marchers and three bands. Directly behind Shelton on his palomino was a car carrying John Bender, who at the time was considered the oldest living pioneer and one of the original permanent settlers. Also with him and in the following two cars were a collection of old-timers and other very early pioneers: Mrs. M.H. LeFetra (arrived here in 1876), Emmett Daugherty (1871), Mrs. Edith Shorey Lee (1880), Mrs. Thomas Kamphefner (1881) and Mrs. Sykes (1881). The comments in the article regarding "original permanent settlers" lends more to folklore than fact, as Daugherty would be the oldest pioneer in the Azusa Valley because Bender (and Cullen) didn't arrive to what would be Glendora until 1874.

Following the pioneers were the Citrus Union High School Band, the American Legion, the Boy Scouts of America and a number of floats and groups from most of the civic organizations in town. There were six categories, replete with winning ribbons and cash prizes (totaling $250).

There were 114 entries for the Golden Get-Together Parade on May 29, 1937, including all three of the fire apparatuses used in Glendora over the years, starting with this horse-drawn pump. The 1915 American LaFrance fire truck can still be seen in Glendora parades to this day.

Glendora's Elementary Schools, with its replica of an early mission, won in the Schools Division and also won the Sweepstakes Cup. Eb's Grocery Store, Glendora's first grocery store and post office, was a float entered by Teter's Market and was awarded most novel float and was also the winner in the Merchants Division.

A distinguished entry (which won the Comic Division) was the history of the Glendora Fire Department. Notable was the 1915 American LaFrance fire truck that can still be seen in today's parades down Glendora Avenue.

A few interesting additions to the parade included a genuine covered wagon pulled by oxen, entered by Walter Cullen (son of William Cullen), and a pair of elephants, entered by H.S. Riser of the Riser Lumber Company. Lambert Whitcomb, the grandson of Glendora's founder, George Whitcomb, was honored as the marshal of the parade (not to be confused with the grand marshal), while they arranged for the "first white child" born in the Azusa Valley, Eta Cullen Reynard, to ride in a float; however, much speculation and debate has occurred over the years concerning this element of the parade. One interesting parade entry was the then seventy-six-year-old Mrs. Francis Reed riding on horseback in an Old West–style saddle, just as she used to do in Glendora fifty years earlier.

All throughout the parade, many of the spectators were wearing felt cowboy hats to set the mood for the Golden Jubilee. The Glendora Museum has two such hats on display in various cases (one with the Sally Rand collection because she had signed it). These hats, along with buttons and souvenir programs, were sold by the hundreds that day. In fact, Eunice Ealy won first prize from Press-Gleaner (publisher of the programs) for selling the most books along the parade route, 105 in total, and they continued to be on sale at Nelson's, Venberg's, the First National Bank, city hall and the newspaper offices for several weeks after the event.

Later on in the afternoon of the twenty-ninth, contests and entertainments were held at the ballpark on North Wabash Avenue, as were various running races (three-legged, for example), a jousting contest and a tug of war.

Veterans of America's wars took an honored place in the parade's lineup.

Between 4:00 and 7:00 p.m. at the City Park, just behind city hall, a barbecue supper was offered, consisting of a "barbecue plate, home-made pie and coffee" for thirty-five cents. Following that at 8:00 p.m. was *The Golden Harvest*, a play written by Henry Scott Rubel and directed by Rachel Graves Smith, telling the story of Glendora's founding. It was staged on the lawn at the Wilson School on the corner of Wabash and Whitcomb Avenues.

Interestingly, at 9:30 p.m., two dances were planned: an "Old Time Dance" was held at 116 North Michigan Avenue, while presumably the younger crowd headed up the street to the Woman's Clubhouse for the "Modern Dance." Either way, one dollar got you and your dancing partner into both doors.

At the tail end of a ten-minute film that has survived all these years, after the crowd had begun to disperse, you can catch a short glimpse of Sam Baxter, who in 1926 was named Glendora's first chief of police and who kept that post until he was replaced in 1948 by O. Dan Fay Jr., son of Dan Fay Sr., who handled crime in Glendora before 1926. Baxter was assisted by Milt Squires as the night watchman in town, and perhaps he is one of the two officers Baxter is speaking to in the film.

Works Consulted

Battler, Bobbie. *Remember When*. Glendora, CA: self-published, 1985.

Bettin, Helen Kennard. *This I Remember: Reminiscences of Old-Timers of Glendora, California*. Glendora, CA: Zephyr Publications, 1990.

Darlington, Kay. *The Making of the Glendora Library from 1903 through 1930*. Glendora, CA: self-published, 1999.

Fracasse, Ida and Joe. *The First 100 Years*. Glendora, CA: Liberty Enterprises, 1986.

Glendora (CA) Gleaner.

Glendora (CA) Press.

Glendoran magazine, 1983–2007. Published in Glendora, California.

Hauser, Ruth. *Keeping the Faith: One Hundred Years*. Glendora, CA: United Methodist Church, 1985.

Hayden, Floyd S. *The History of Citrus Union High School and Junior College.* Vol. 1, *1891–1922.* Azusa, CA: Azusa Herald and Pomotropic, 1952.

Jackson, Sheldon G. *Beautiful Glendora: Its People and History.* Azusa, CA: Azusa Pacific University Press, 1982.

————. *A British Ranchero in Old California: The Life and Times of Henry Dalton and the Rancho Azusa.* Glendale, CA: Arthur H. Clark Company, 1987.

Pflueger, Donald H. *Glendora.* Glendora, CA: Sauders Press, 1951.

Traversi, David C. *One Man's Dream: The Spirit of the Rubel Castle.* Glendora, CA: Strange Publications, 2002.

About the Author

Ryan Lee Price moved to Glendora with his family at the age of three and spent the next thirty-five years discovering the many joys of growing up in such a wonderful town. Ryan currently lives in Corona, California, with his wife, Kara, and their two children, Natalie and Matthew. He is the author of two automotive history and restoration books for antique Volkswagen enthusiasts, and his articles appear regularly in a wide range of monthly publications. He is very involved in the Glendora Historical Society and has a passion for the history of his hometown. This is his second book on Glendora's history.

Visit us at
www.historypress.net